Listen to Our Lady
Or Go to Hell

Father Christopher Riehl

Edited by Nathaniel Slattery

Cover design by Nathaniel Slattery

ISBN: 979-8-9868167-1-5

*For Our Lady, Saint Joseph, Saint Michael, Saint Augustine,
Saint Thomas Aquinas, Saint Jerome,
Saint Louis-Marie de Montfort, and Saint Christopher*

For the salvation of souls

Editor's Note

By the grace of God, you are about to read a book that is comprehensive, penetrating, insightful, and terrifying.

Father Riehl is a good and holy priest, recognized by everyone as suited for leadership in the Church. He possesses the virtues of courage, wisdom, and magnanimity in the correct proportions, at least from my humble lay point of view, in order to revivify and renew a diocese. Likely, in a just and ordered society, he would be a bishop shortly, and this is exactly what he would be doing. He would be extracting his body, mind, heart, and soul of all of its energy and capacity, jogging from one end of the diocese to the other, and removing every semblance and hair of error from every corner such that the faithful could look and see nearly the spotless Bride of Christ within his diocese, or until he collapsed. But this would necessarily involve ruffling many feathers, not lay so much as clerical, and no doubt very, very many people would be removed by the gravity of their errors. That is why he is not a bishop and very likely never will be before Our Lady triumphs. He is exactly the type of person that intimidates the type of priest with which most people live.

Maybe I don't know him well enough, maybe I am transported with joy at finding more than a single holy priest (my own parish has a holy priest who knew that his job was to provide the Sacraments these last couple of years), maybe I am a dirty flatterer (pray God no), but this is what I see. We live in such a time, bathed by oceans of infant blood, steeped in the darkness once reserved for homosexual relations before they were allowed to speak up near the altar on Father's Day in a Catholic Church in Chicago, and under the boot of our Nominalist overlords, that we don't deserve priests and bishops and popes that remove error and dispel confusion. We have ancestors that for hundreds of years have likely prayed that their progeny would not convert to Catholicism. We have the pride to judge God Himself, and we blaspheme the Holy Ghost to pass the time in our boredom. We live under curses, justly earned, and so we live under poor shepherds.

But God still creates these men in the womb and suckles them in the Sacraments, because His Glory and Holiness are too intoxicating to allow it not to happen. So they exist, and what He seems to do is this: prevent them from having any authority, hide them away from the world that hates Him, and let them do other things than help save people who don't deserve it.

That is what Father Riehl is. He is a good and holy man, who with all of the capacity and virtue of a saintly bishop in the chrysalis, has instead written a humble book, and now we can read it. He may not be suited for writing, which is good, because it is tiresome to read pretty words that say nothing, and those types of books and documents are easy enough to find within the Church. He is suited for salvation and sanctification.

Here is how to approach this book:

I said it is comprehensive. It is. It spans history from the pagan Greeks and Romans to 2019, touching and illuminating philosophy, showing Our Lady's apparitions in their correct context, and explaining why Heaven, Hell, and the Earth have been doing and saying the things they have for three thousand years. Therefore, approach the book patiently, and be willing to continue along until the end, and then go back to understand things which you did not understand at first. It is remarkably concise for the timespan.

I said this book is penetrating. It is. You will likely encounter some of your own false beliefs. I, for one, misunderstood what the virtue of obedience is in such a way as has sent men to Hell since at least World War II. So when you encounter these, have recourse to prayer, and do not be afraid to put the book down and consult Our Lord and Our Lady for a moment. If you are moved to the Sacraments, to Confession, then Father Riehl would be delighted, I am sure.

I said this book is insightful. It is. Near the end, particularly, he makes many insights and comments which are fascinating, meaning that they may fasten you to him. But rather, see that it is a love and interest in Our Lady, and a sincere desire to do as She says, that makes Father Riehl who he is, and strive to emulate him.

I said that this book is terrifying. It is. One hundred years ago, Our Lady said it is too late. When you read this book, the just understanding is that the Lord ought to sack this whole world and start over again, and who can blame Him? But don't let this lead you into despair. Let it lead you into love of the Lord. What mercy He has! And He gives endless roads to sanctity for us. The ultimate goal of this book is revealed in a tiny line: We need saints more than ever— why not you?

Don't skip over this pithy little comment of Father's. This is the crux of the book. There is no hope in the world anyways, and so pursuit of sanctity is beyond reasonable. But more important than that, with how bad everything is, it has never been easier to be one! Thank the Lord that He reveals things to you, because simply to be beyond the confusion of things is a sure sign of His particular Love. So take this invitation very seriously. Find out how to be one, and then be one. Stop sinning, study virtue, read the saints, pray endlessly, do penance, and find Hope, true Hope, theological Hope, which stands like a glorious angel over the bound devil of worldly hope.

—Nathaniel Slattery, Editor

Table of Contents

Introduction

The following is a collection of chapters on the current situation in the world and the Church, what it is, a brief history of how we got here, and the beginning of a solution to love and know God better and dwell with Him after death, despite all of the charms and temptations of this most corrupt world and society. This is the purpose of human existence. Here I take for granted that this life is a time of transition which is short. How can we measure 100 years in comparison to eternity? I also take for granted that life as we know it is clouded by the effects of original sin. The ultimate effect is death. Until death, we have to deal with a weakened will, a darkened intellect, and a tendency to choose poorly called concupiscence. This is true for all of fallen mankind.

You may ask, "What is your point?" The point is that our loving God has not left us in this state without His assistance. He has sent His Son to enter among us as a man, be like us in all things but sin, and to suffer and die for us. He has accomplished all this, and thus we have a way to get to the peace and joy for which we long; a peace and joy of which we only receive small glimpses in this life. These small glimpses are called graces. They are gifts He gave us, and they make us more and more like His Son who dwelt among us. Grace builds on nature. The more we receive these graces, the more we become like Him so that eventually we can say, like St. Paul, Gal 2:20 "And I live, now not I: but Christ liveth in me." Thus when the Father looks on us, He sees His Son in us and loves us. NB: All Biblical quotes taken from the Douay-Rheims translation of the Vulgate.

The Lord created man so that we could learn about God and thus could love Him. You cannot love what you do not know. By learning to love Him we can then one day be with Him and see Him as He truly is. But how are we to learn about Him? He has given us a society to faithfully hand on the truths that He taught to his disciples when He was alive. This is the Church, and it is called the Perfect Society. It is perfect in the sense that the Lord is present and guiding His people and perfecting the members of this group until they are ready to join Him in paradise.

The problem is, as St. John says in his Gospel, Jn 3:19: "the light is come into the world and men loved darkness rather than the light: for their works were evil." This conflict or fight between the light and the darkness is all around us. In our time a kind of eclipse of the light of Christ has made it even more difficult to see the path toward God. Just as a physician cannot accurately treat an ailment unless he knows the origin of it, so too we will not be able to heal the society of our time, unless we know the origin of the ailment. Hence this little book.

Nemo dat quod non habet. You cannot give what you do not have. This book is an attempt to show the history of thought that has led to the current way of thinking which is most prevalent today. Ideas have consequences and, while we see the consequences every day, it is helpful to know the origins so that we can deal with them more successfully.

Our situation: Christendom destroyed; Modernism reigning supreme

The society exists principally to help the individual, and the body politic exists to ensure the optimal situation for everyone to pursue God. Our society or civilization, known as "the West", was once known as Christendom because it had God and the pursuit of Him as the basic premise for daily life. It has been destroyed. This neither came about quickly nor easily, but the current situation is very much opposed to the principles of Christendom and continues to vigorously destroy any remaining vestiges of this lost society.

Some of the marks of the current times are Nominalism, Modernism, Materialism, Egoism, Rationalism, Relativism, and the like. Modernism has been spoken of as the synthesis of all errors. Of course, this is most pointedly seen in the realm of the faith. Heresies of every kind and new combinations of them have exploded in the world, while the old heresies continue to attack the same old targets: the Incarnation, Hypostatic Union, Virgin Birth, Real Presence, Triune God, nature and goodness of God, One Holy Apostolic Church, modes of salvation and grace, final judgment, clerical state and life, the hierarchical nature of Creation, angels and demons, the existence of Hell, and many more doctrines. These have all been attacked, creating confusion presently, and there have been times of confusion in regards to these and other points in the past. But what is new with Modernism is a sustained and prolific attack on Sacred Tradition, and as some state, at the same time, infiltration into the clerical ranks by enemies of God and the Church. These are men who not only do not believe the Creed but actively work to undermine it.

The Faith is absolute; the New Covenant was ratified by Our dear Lord in His Holy Passion and by the sending of the Holy Ghost, which also at Pentecost perfected the Church, which is the society of believers established from the Side of Christ on the Cross. All these things are cast into confusion by Modernism. It has become so bad that there are a great many priests which do not believe, understand, nor even know the Faith in its most basic sense. For example, it is easy to find a priest agreeing with the statements: "You don't need to go to Confession", "Angels don't exist", "If there is a Hell, dare we assume and hope that there is nobody in it?", etc. You can find many clerics changing the very simple formula for Baptism so much that the people they baptize then have to be found and baptized correctly. There are many more examples. In a better time, no one would have been allowed to receive the Blessed Sacrament for the first time unless they knew and believed the basic truths questioned today.

Separation of faith and reason leads to separation of Church from our lives

Pope Benedict XVI gave a presentation on September 12, 2006 at the University of Regensburg, Germany, where he had been a professor when he was a young priest. It was about the separation of faith and reason, and he started with a dialogue which the Emperor of Byzantium had with a muslim at the end of the 14th century. He showed that the muslims had separated faith and reason and thus could do things in the name of their religion that went against reason.

In the *Euthyphro* dialogue, Plato (437-347 BC) poses the following question: "Is something good because God wills it or does God will something because it is good?" Most philosophers, including St. Thomas Aquinas, affirm the latter, but divine command theorists or Nominalists affirm the former. This creates an obedience that is blind and a rule that is tyrannical.

Pope Benedict XVI goes on to point out that this happened again during the "Middle Ages" when the protestants also separated faith and reason. This then leads to the separation of higher and lower sciences. Science is the systematic study of something, the lower sciences concerned with the physical universe (math, physics, biology, chemistry, etc.), and the higher sciences concerned with the metaphysical, beyond the physical (i.e. philosophy and theology). As with faith and reason, the lower and higher are separated. This separation has been used to present the lower sciences as the only enlightened study that is worthy of man and as resulting in the general betterment of life as we know it. In this schema any study of the higher sciences is not science at all and is in fact merely superstition and myth.

The resultant separation of faith and reason has led the majority of people to ignore the clear teachings of the Church or to simply categorize these teachings as opinion. Further, by ignoring the supernatural order of creation, it attempts to replace God with man. This is the same reasoning that led to the Fall in the Garden. "If you eat, you will be likened unto God." This is nonsense because the end or purpose of a thing is determined by its creator, not by the thing created. How could a finite mortal become an infinite God by simply eating something?

Here we can see the dichotomy of faith and reason results in a lack of clear and consistent thought. For example, these days a common line of thinking from the mouth of a politician is: "I think it's wrong to do this or that, but if they want to, it's okay." The same conclusion was made by the muslims centuries ago. You can do irrational things, even acts that go contrary to your own ethics, if it is willed by God, or by some other higher power.

On the other hand, if theology can and does say something real about life then you are compelled to live and choose according to it. For example; the Church has revealed that all men are made in the image and likeness of God, therefore all human life is of value and should be respected, and we cannot murder regardless if a person is suffering and has a low chance of survival. However, if you hold that faith is irrational then it is of no concern to ignore it or to silence the voice of the Church. By this logic, if it is irrational it should be silenced.

Silencing of the Church leads to Materialism and Egoism

If faith and reason are totally separate and only reason is grounded in reality then all you truly know is based on the physical/material world. Materialism is the basic principle that man can be fulfilled by pursuing materialistic ends as a means and end of life which promises happiness, or even more destructive, that the material/physical world is all that exists. Many have been led to perdition by this denial of the supernatural and preternatural aspects of reality. There have been many proponents of this perversion: at the top of the list; Descartes, Kant, Darwin, Marx, Freud, Loisy, Tyrrell, and Teilhard de Chardin. These, it seems, have had a great deal of influence on the common thoughts of people today.

Materialism has also put forward the ridiculous notion of evolution. Evolution is the idea that a lower and less sophisticated creature will, over time, develop into a more complex creature by a "natural" process of selection. This theory begs the question, if this "law of nature" is true, where did it come from? The reality of entropy has always been seen and proven to be true. How could a lower being or thing somehow jump or change to be a more complex being or thing on its own? Logically, only a more complex being can change or manipulate a simpler thing into a thing more complex.

If it is the case that the only thing real in the universe is what is physical, and you are the judge of what is true, then Egoism is the result. Egoism is the general notion that man, or an individual man, is his own judge and arbiter of what he may or may not do in any given situation to advance his own interests. Man-centered life is the essence of egoism. The result is the separation of man from a community or society in general. It could be summed up with the statement, "if it makes you happy, it can't be that bad." Thus you, so long as you agreed, would be free to act. The point is that if the Church has nothing real to say, it must be silenced. The problem is that where the Church goes, so goes the World. Are we then all silently being led to perdition?

Man-centered thinking is realized in Romanticism and lack of logic

To all of this we can add the terrible philosophy of Romanticism. Romanticism is simply the idea that: 1. There is no interplay between faith and reason. That is, that ultimately there is not a logical reason or explanation for faith; and 2. Because of this the only thing left for faith is the experience of it. That is, the emotions and so forth that come from faith or a religious experience is the whole of it. You can see this so often these days when people will ask each other how they felt or thought about a mass, homily, etcYou are supposed to go to Mass to offer to God what is His due, thanksgiving and sacrifice for what He has already and continues to do for us.

The emphasis on feelings is very often to the detriment of the higher faculties, and it has reduced much human behavior to little different from the actions of irrational beasts. Now, the majority of people live based on the idea of Immanentism. This is different than the Divine Immanence, which is the reality that at the same time God is present in a special way to everyone that is in a state of grace, but also, at the same time, infinitely transcendent of Creation. Immanentism is the idea that anyone who believes in or accepts that God is God, is also individually the judge and arbiter of all revealed truth. You run into this frequently when a statement about a simple traditional teaching of the Church will not be believed by someone until they have read the source for themselves and judged it.

Some ecclesiastics decades ago noted that they had witnessed the end of the "liberal" time and that they saw the ushering in of the time of religion. By this they meant that the liberal time is marked by the acceptance and actualization of rebellion. Hidden behind the facade of, "I'm okay; you're okay," is a more sinister plot to make the only standard of society a personal judgment. The "liberals" at first fought against the rulers of a particular place and against the institutions in society that helped those rulers stay as rulers. In the current time, with almost all those institutions either destroyed outright or weakened to the point that they are practically non-existent, the rebellion has reached its final enemy: the assault against the very one that put those institutions in place, namely God. This is what those ecclesiastics meant. The people of this time would not hold typical religious views, to know and learn about God. Rather they would have made themselves or their ideas into gods. And further they are incredibly militant against anyone who even speaks against their ideology. They work tirelessly to destroy any dissenters or heretics to their beliefs. Today it is called the "cancel culture" or "woke culture". It is a man-made religion, and all dissenters must be crushed.

Failure of clear objective thinking results in the dictatorship of Relativism

The final result of the current situation is what Pope Benedict XVI called the "dictatorship of Relativism". This dictatorship is another way of explaining the demand for orthodoxy to follow the ideas of this religion, which is Egoism, Materialism, etc. Simply call it Modernism. The dictatorship reveals itself in an absolute demand that everyone follow the modern creed.

This is not the first time that the Church has had to deal with other religions. A more notable attack was the protestant revolt of recent memory, of which we are still dealing with the fallout. And it is striking how there are many similarities between today and the 16th century. In both cases the Church had internal and external factors working against the clear and Divine mandate to go and make disciples of all men, thereby freely giving the means of salvation to the world. In both cases the outer visible enemies of the Gospel were backed by governments and their agents, as well as private individuals. In both cases the largest problems for the Church were and are inflicted from within, not without.

In the very life of Our Lord, He fortified the faith of His Apostles before sending them out. The healing of the Church in the past started with a fortification of the priesthood, shared quickly with a fortification of the family. This was accomplished down the centuries by more clear teaching of the truths of that same faith given to the Apostles. At the time of the Council of Trent, (1545-63) the major fortification or renewal was principally a renewal of the hierarchy and clear teaching on it. Thankfully we still have those clear teachings from the Council of Trent as a blueprint for clerical renewal.

It is true that a similar renewal is needed in the current crisis. However, I think the thing we must keep in mind is that the Lord came to save individual people. Yes, we are a corporate and worldwide society, but fundamentally the Gospel, conversion, and the graces given in the Sacraments are dispensed by a one on One basis. In contrast to this is the opposing dictatorship that is based on the creed in which only subjective (individual) truths are real. Of course this makes no sense. The only rule is the rule I make up. But what if my rule contradicts your rule. Can two opposing rules both be right? No.

The Queen of Heaven has a response

We would be fools if we did not mention Our Lady. She has been calling people to conversion and being faithful to the Gospel for millennia, all the while warning people of the immediate need for prayer and penance. In these recent times she has been particularly warning of a Chastisement that would be more severe than the deluge of the Great Flood. In times past, say when Christendom still existed, Our Lord passed His reminders throughout the hierarchy, but at Fatima she was speaking directly to the faithful. Some of the reasons are obvious to us now. The confidence and trust the laity have in the hierarchy in general has been severely eroded. More than that, I believe the Lord has willed these apparitions to highlight the central role Our Queen should have in our lives.

While the Blessed Mother should be involved in every individual's life, it would be good to reflect on the larger results of the attacks of these recent times on the people in general. It was often ruefully noted at the turn of the last century how the loss of reason and the higher faculties were at that time resulting in an ever increasing difficulty to explain how these terrible notions would result in a situation like today. If we could take the minds of people formed in a Christian society and bring them to our time, it would be easy to simply point out and remind them of the Church's teaching. However, we have to deal with minds that were not only illogically formed but most often hardened against clear thinking and reason. What is worse, this includes not only the laity and nonbelievers, but a good number of the hierarchy. We have been called and now commissioned to do our utmost to be agents of salvation to them all. It seems the hardest people to call to true conversion are former, inactive Catholics, but actually the most difficult would be non-believing priests and bishops.

In the end one might say that the true loss today is of a sense of the transcendent, the supernatural. As Pope St. Pius X pointed out, when the modernists modified the Catholic understanding of God they made everyone into little gods. The promise is now fulfilled that was made by the serpent in the Garden. On the other hand, we can choose to embrace the supernatural, all-powerful God that took pity on us fallen men. He created the perfect and true tabernacle of the Lord by saving Our Lady from sin, which is the Immaculate Conception, and thus made ready for the incarnation of the Divine Logos, Him we call Jesus the Christ, Savior of the World, King of the Universe.

I have attempted to write the remaining chapters in a linear, historical way up to the present time. The next chapter will be a quick overview of philosophy in the time of the ancient Greeks to the Council of Trent. This work is mostly about some of the bad ideas that continue to be kicked around today. My *modus operandi* is that of a physician trying to find the sources of the cancers we see so prevalent in our time. I find many good people talking about the cancers but not getting to the root of them. By treating the symptoms there will be no real and lasting cure. My goal is deeper. I hope and pray this little contribution is of some help to someone.

Chapter 1
How did we get here? Part One
From the Ancient Greeks to the Council of Trent

We have pondered the situation in brief in the above section, that is, both the situation we are in and the history and origins of it. Now we ought to reflect at length on the path that has led this previously Christian society to the point which we are at now. We will begin with the ancient Romans and Greeks, who we will see not only invented all of the incorrect ideas that plague us today, but also ultimately rejected those ideas in favor of Christendom and truth. After the establishment of Christendom, things nevertheless slowly break down, first in a rejection of the Pope by schismatics, next in a rejection of the Church by heretics, and finally in a rejection of all authority but his own by the English King. Heaven responds by sending Our Lady, and the Church responds with the Council of Trent. We will finish by examining a seed of later problems after the Council of Trent, which is changes in the idea of obedience. History repeats itself.

Ancient Greeks/Romans, faith, reason, freedom, and virtue
    Let us start then with the materialists. In pre-Christian times, Greeks named Leucippus and Democritus the atomist, tried to reduce the explanation of the universe to atoms. Everything is made of atoms. There is nothing else. Another Greek, Epicurus, still influential today, taught a moral Relativism in which the lower sciences were only useful because they destroyed belief in the transcendent and supernatural, an early attack on faith. For him only the material was real, everything else was myth and superstition. He separated faith and reason. Thus he "freed" himself from transcendent truths and was then able to pursue pleasure for its own sake and avoid pain, which he considered the only true evil. He is said to be the father of naturalistic science, in which bound the natural sciences are bound to a philosophy.
    In Epicurus's model, the lower sciences go beyond their proper area of study and inquiry. Properly speaking, the lower sciences are a study of the material world by observation and hypotheses. He tried to argue metaphysical positions based on the lower sciences. Metaphysical means beyond the physical senses.

12

An example of this is arguments supporting homosexual lifestyles as being based on "science", such as the "homosexual gene" or the statement that "they were born that way". The arguments continue despite the proofs utterly failing. These arguments are philosophical in nature but clearly beyond the scope of the lower sciences, and still, "science" is said to be the basis for the argument.

A Roman, Lucretius, advanced Materialism. He came up with an idea of the origin of the universe and all creatures in it from random processes separate from intelligent design. He anticipated the idea of "survival of the fittest" as a philosophical necessity to keep the dream of his materialist forbears alive. If a "natural process" explained the world, then faith is nonsense, and Materialism wins.

Aristotle opposes Materialism by his principles. In *Physics* II 3 and *Metaphysics* V 2, Aristotle offers his general account of the four causes of anything. This account is general in the sense that it applies to everything that requires an explanation, including artistic production and human action. Here Aristotle recognizes four answers that can be given to a why-question:

- The material cause: "that out of which", e.g., the bronze of a statue.
- The formal cause: "the form", "the account of what-it-is-to-be", e.g., the shape of a statue.
- The efficient cause: "the primary source of the change or rest", e.g., the artisan, the art of bronze-casting the statue, the man who gives advice, the father of the child.
- The final cause: "the end, that for the sake of which a thing is done", e.g., health is the end of walking, losing weight, purging, drugs, and surgical tools.

All the four kinds of causes may enter into the explanation of something. Consider the production of an artifact like a bronze statue. The bronze enters into the explanation of the production of the statue as *the material cause*. Note that the bronze is not only the material out of which the statue is made; it is also the subject of change, that is, the thing that undergoes the change and results in a statue. The bronze is melted and poured in order to acquire a new shape, the shape of the statue. This shape enters into the

explanation of the production of the statue as *the formal cause*.
However, an adequate explanation of the production of a statue
requires also a reference to *the efficient cause* or the principle that
produces the statue. For Aristotle, this principle is the art of
bronze-casting the statue.[i]

The Romans weren't buying Materialism either. The Fathers
of the Church knew these philosophers well. To oppose them, the
Fathers explained creation in conformity with the Sacred Text and
right reason. St. Jerome, St. Augustine, St. Hippolytus, Dionysus
the Great, and Lactantius wrote against Materialism, teaching the
reality of Divine Providence. Man and the universe originated
according to the Divine plan and Holy Will of God.

The errors of these pre-Christian philosophers quickly fell
away but then were brought back in the middle and late 15th
century. Their reemergence was an element of Rationalism, the
philosophical underpinning of Luther and the like that arose after
1517.

The Greeks, Romans, and Fathers of the Church dismissed
these arguments for Materialism. The very order of the world, and
the order and complexity of man, points to intelligent design.
Further, man has the capacity to know himself, other men, and the
world. This capacity points to a possibility to know beyond the
world of men, the supernatural. The Greeks called it the "unknown
God". This God was free and shared His freedom with man and
gave him the ability to become better, to be a better man. This is
the root of virtue, manliness. Choosing the good, avoiding evil, and
over time becoming more good.

In opposition, the attempt to separate faith and reason is as old
as recorded, advanced intellectual thought. The motivation is
universal license to do self-centered acts.

We'll take God, Christ, the Church, but leave the Pope

Diocletian reformed the Roman Empire and split the
governance of it into East and West in 286 AD, before Constantine
the Great allowed Christianity to be legal in the Edict of Milan,
313 AD, and returned confiscated lands and goods to the
Christians. The separate governance of the Eastern and Western
Empires continued until the West practically collapsed in 476 AD
and the court in Ravenna was dissolved in 554 AD. At this time the

Pope was the ruler of Rome and much of middle Italy. The East, called Byzantium, continued until 1453 AD when Constantinople fell to the muslims.

During the course of this history, the two halves of the Empire slowly separated politically, economically, and religiously. In the East, the Church was always closely tied to the state, even subordinate. However, in Rome and the West, the popes have always fought vigorously for the freedoms of the Church, even sometimes being bullied, as by Napoleon, but they were largely able to stay free of state control. Beyond this, the philosophy, theology, and liturgy between East and West had largely different points of emphasis, resulting in two similar but distinct cultures. Yes, both were Christians with Apostolic roots, but they were growing apart.

The closeness of the Church in the Eastern Empire to the State led to some conflicts that were theological, philosophical, and political. A lack of clear communication and fraternal charity at times led to disputes which would have otherwise been avoidable. The various heresies that both assailed the East and often came from the East led to a distancing and cooling of formerly close ties. As the Papacy grew into its own in terms of prestige and power, there was a natural distancing and even fear of the Eastern Emperors for their perceived privileges and control of the Church in the East. These tensions, combined with some distinct personalities, led to a mutual excommunication in 1054 AD, called the Great Schism.

The Easterners left full communion— or they were kicked out, depending on your point of view. They took God, Christ, and the Church, and they left the pope. Here I mean the hierarchical nature of the Church— bishop, priest, etc.— was retained, but there was no visible head, the pope.

The oft-made argument is that the pope is merely one of the Patriarchs. This presupposes that the Lord left the flock without a shepherd. Or are we to think that the Lord wants a democracy of shepherds? The worst way to lead an army is with a cadre of generals; the best run ships have a single captain; the One Church must be unified under one head. This will be very important for the history of the 20th and 21st centuries.

Finally, it should be noted that despite the Great Schism in 1054, the Schismatics and Catholics still got along. For example, the many Crusades were in large part to defend Byzantium from muslim aggression, as well as protect the rest of Europe. And despite the theological and political disagreements, the Christians also unified in defense during the Mongol invasions of the 13th century.

Let's take God and Christ, but leave the Church and the Pope

In 1517, a disgruntled priest named Fr. Martin Luther wrote his complaints out, and he, or one of his students, put them on the front of the local church in Germany.

The fundamental difficulty for him was a misunderstanding of grace. Grace is a favor, the free and undeserved help that God gives us to respond to His call to become children of God, adoptive sons, partakers of the Divine Nature and of eternal life. Holy Mother Church teaches that grace builds on nature. This means that even as we are born with original sin and not His children, He calls us to be His children and then makes us His adopted children. This is more than a legal decree (John Calvin) and more than a covering us over (Martin Luther). It is an actual change in our very being. We call this sanctifying grace. It makes us more like Him: holy and sanctified. Grace raises us fallen men into the state that God had originally planned for us.

Because the Lord is all-knowing, perfect, etc., He never goes against His rules and laws, as Luther and Calvin suggest. For instance, Luther had a problem with the Priesthood of Christ because he thought that all of created matter was corrupt and thus evil. How could the Divine Logos, the perfect Wisdom and Creator of all things, take on flesh, or even act through the corrupted flesh after His Ascension? How could He go against Himself? For Luther, because of the filth of created matter, he had to reject grace changing anything. For him, grace covered over the nastiness. Thus, when God looked down at us, He saw a covering over of our filth; did not see our filth, and thereby accepted us.

No. Luther was wrong; God fulfills the plan, the path that He had always marked out for us. Thus miracles are not the suspension of God's laws or in any way against His rules; rather they are a bringing forth, a showing of His plans and His ways. You can think of it as a little glimpse behind the veil that hides His awe-inspiring nature to varying degrees. We will see in later chapters a few of the miracles Our Lord, through Our Lady, has revealed to the world.

Luther's theology was the opposite of what the Lord Himself revealed. The Lord said that He would leave us a way to actually commune, to be one with Him physically. He gave us Himself in the Most Blessed Sacrament, a perpetuation of His perfect sacrifice on the Cross. This, of course, requires a method of perpetuation. Thus, He gave us a share in His Priesthood, both in a general way, the priesthood of believers, but also in a specific way, the ministerial, sacred Priesthood. In the sacraments of Baptism, Confirmation, and Holy Orders, the very essence of the soul is changed and sanctified. In Orders, the soul is changed in a particular way to be able to act *in persona Christi*, in the person of Christ. In this way, the Lord acts in and through the hands and body of the priest to make Himself present in the Eucharist. But the protestants rejected the priesthood, and thus rejected the Church.

Without bishops, who make priests, there is no church in the real sense. Bishops and priests are the shepherds. Or are we to imagine that the sheep shepherd themselves? Maybe the sheep vote for one of their own number to be the head sheep? I am sure sheep do not act in this way. It is more likely that when the Lord used all of those parables of the sheep, He was referring to the basic structure of the Church. It follows that the Apostles thought the same thing, because they did set the Church up that way.

In the end, the protestants took only God and Christ. They needed a way of knowing Christ, and so they invented *sola scripture*. Thus, they kept the books written and brought together by the Church, but left the Church, with its hierarchy and the pope.

One final note: I would argue that without cheap books the very notion of *sola sciptura* is impossible. Up until Luther, books of all kinds were terribly expensive. With the advent of the printing press, that changed.. How could God join belief and understanding of Him to the printed word when, for a millennia and a half after the Resurrection, only the wealthiest had access to books? Or is salvation reserved to the rich? Or do the poor simply have to trust the rich?

If you don't let me marry her, or maybe her … or her…. I'll just take over the Church

In the revolt of King Henry VIII of England 1534, Henry made himself the head of the protestant "church of England". Not being satisfied with placing himself on equal rank with the successor of St. Peter, he claimed an absolute right called "the divine right of kings", claiming it directly from God. He was the first to make this ridiculous assertion. This is a perversion of the Catholic teaching that all authority comes from God through the pope and down to bishops, priests, kings, princes, and so forth. His version had himself answerable to no one. Must be nice. Henry and his merry band stole vast amounts of land and sacred objects from the Church, kicking out, arresting, and even killing the priests and religious that tried to oppose him. In their drunken zeal for theft, these fools also destroyed the most advanced furnace in existence, recently developed and built by some monks, and which could create primitive steel. This set the development of that metal back hundreds of years.

This version of absolute authority which King Henry invented was based on Nominalism and called "divine command theory". If the king had his authority directly from God and any command given by the king is a good command, then doing anything the king commands is good. Thus, off with her head! Oh, and hers, too.

The truly sad thing about this wayward king is that, just a few years before he separated from the Church, he was actually defending Her from the likes of Luther and others. He had been named a "Defender of the Faith" by the Pope. His difficulty was that he really desired a son who would be able to succeed him. In his mind, the problem was with his wife, so he wanted a new wife. The reality is that the Church had no power to dissolve the union of husband and wife: "What God has joined let no man put asunder", but he left the Church and had his lackeys declare that he was never married. He then went through six women, including his true wife, who gave him some daughters and then a son. Some of the women he executed; one died after childbirth.

The ironic thing about this story is that now we know it is from the father that either a boy or girl issues. It was not his many wives' faults. In any event, many historians believe that, without the schism of Henry, the protestants could have never lasted in mainland Europe.

Apostasy is the rejection of the teachings of the Church, a renunciation of the Faith. Schism is when you leave unity with the Church, which is usually a rejection of the authority of the Pope.

Heresy is the picking and choosing of some of the teachings of the Church while rejecting others. Integral Catholic Faith is the adherence and belief in everything the Church teaches and everything for which the Church calls.

The Lord responds by sending His Mother, and the Council of Trent

In December 1531, Our Lady responded to the desperate prayers of the Bishop of Mexico City.

He and his priests were having a very difficult time converting the native peoples and governing the military personnel in Mexico. Some shameful abuses of the indigenous peoples had developed that concerned the priests and bishop, and they were at their wits' end. The bishop turned to Our Lady for help. Our Lady appeared to a local man, and, through him, the image of Our Lady of Guadalupe was given to the world.

We don't have the space to get into all the wonderful aspects of this apparition, but let's look at it in the larger context. At the same time in which hundreds of thousands of Catholics were losing the faith in Europe and more than a century of serious fighting, wars, famines, and like were inflicting Europe, on the other side of the Earth, Our Lady appears. It seems so simple, but, within a couple decades, it has been calculated that over ten million people of the New World had joined the Church. In terms of conversions, Our Lady of Guadalupe has no equal. She is the patroness of the Americas.

The Council of Trent in northern Italy (1545-1563) was the 19th ecumenical council. It dealt with the lack of discipline in the clergy and gave some clarifications on the dogmas of the Faith that were being disputed at the time. It also gave a more uniform cohesion to the celebration of the Sacraments throughout the Roman Catholic Church. One of the interesting things about the Council is the seeming lack of enthusiasm for it. Almost twenty years in which, for many years, no one even met? One of the popes during this time didn't think it was even needed and thus did not allow anyone to meet. He was concerned with the threat of the muslims coming and conquering, taking slaves and the like.

Nonetheless, Trent was a needed council and brought a new sense of order out of the disorder and lack of discipline that had preceded it. One of the effects of the council that we still see today is the rise of the Catholic education system, seminaries and universities. They existed before, but now they would multiply and spread the availability of higher education, also helped by books being much less expensive.

Does obedience really mean that I can't think anymore?

There is one more aspect of the so called "Counter Reformation", also called the "Catholic Reformation", which will help us understand our current crisis. It is a question about law, authority, and obedience. Already we have seen that Nominalism proposes divine command theory. This theory states that whatever the authority commands is good. He could command murder, idolatry, sodomy, or anything else, and refusing these actions would be evil. As authority is handed down from God to the pope, bishops, religious superiors, priests, kings, princes, and so forth, then, with a strict application of this principle, you could be commanded to do anything and would be obliged to do so. How did this idea get into the Church? Nominalism was largely repudiated by St. Thomas Aquinas, but some elements remained after the Council of Trent.

St. Ignatius of Loyola, founder of the Society of Jesus (Jesuits), has a famous teaching on obedience. We don't have the space here for a full treatise, but we can get the high points. For St. Thomas Aquinas, obedience is the execution of an order given by a superior, so long as it is lawful and possible. (A superior can't order you to swim from NY to London, even as it breaks no moral or legal code directly). St. Ignatius agrees with this but goes on to say that you must conform your will and intellect to the superior to the point that the will and intellect are sacrificed at the altar of obedience. Someone who lives under obedience is to be carried and directed by Divine Providence through the agency of the superior, as if he were a lifeless body. The members of the Jesuits certainly took a literal approach to this instruction. See Fr. Alphonsus Rodriguez SJ's *Practice of Perfection and Christian Virtues,* 1609, that was required reading for novices until the second Vatican council. In this treatise it is stated that what was required was obedience to the superior to the point that if an act is bad or evil, then it will not be counted against you. Rather, the superior will be held accountable.

The rather rigid notion of obedience which St. Ignatius held seems to have been intended by the saint for the formation of new men, but, after they had been thoroughly formed into a Jesuit, they would no longer act in this manner. It sounds a lot like the training in the military, and, indeed, before founding the Jesuits, St. Ignatius had spent all his life in the military.

It is reasonable to say, in opposition to Fr. Rodriguez above, that the disposition which the saint suggests, obedience to a superior as if he were God, is meant to be an internal mode rather than a literal one. There is a parallel. After the famous thirty day retreat which is the start of Jesuit training, they spend a week in a Benedictine monastery. This is as if to say that the outward obedience given to the Abbot and the Prior of the monastery every day is to be internalized for the Jesuit. Especially during the life of St. Ignatius, where the main work of the Jesuits was missionary work, usually only a few Jesuits were ever together out "in the field". Thus, a literal day to day obedience is only possible for a Jesuit while he is still in formation (school).

However, while I think my little explanation is plausible, the reason I bring this up is that the literal approach is often the disposition of people in the Church today. Both clerics and laymen will often say, "Well, my bishop told me to do this," or not to do that, or, "My priest said it was okay". The Nominalist idea of divine command frees the person of actual responsibility. This is, of course, a lie. We are told time and again that bad priests drag many souls down with them to perdition. The defense that "I was ordered to do this" did not work at the Nuremberg trials and won't work in front of the Tribunal of God, either.

It would be good to note that this idea of law, authority, and obedience became very prevalent in the Church after Trent. The application of this servile obedience formed in the clergy is a recipe that destroyed character and the capacity for independent thought. It resulted in a pride in submission, and as life in this mode of tyranny is always looking outward, then any true self-reflection or -criticism, let alone a healthy criticism of clerical life, is stamped out. Further, that the superiors that inflict this training and life have all been "raised up" in it, means that those who do advance are those most adept in the arts of the slave: flattery, dissimulation, manipulation, punishment, and destruction of non-conformists. Sadly, this system which does not give reasons for orders, and does not answer questions for the reasons, forms men that tend to also blindly give and receive orders. Young men of low or malleable character, self-confidence, and intelligence, tend to do well in this environment. Men with opposite traits tend to suffer.

One last thing to note is that St. Ignatius required his men to disclose their consciences to superiors twice a year. It is like a full confession without absolution. We can call it a blurring of the lines between the internal (Sacramental Confession) and external (regular life). The conversations within Confession are forbidden to be spoken of or even hinted at by the priest, but here they are not only shared between superiors, they are used for assignments and more. If you thought an environment of servile obedience was bad, imagine adding to it that your superiors know everything in your conscience. I think Marx and Lenin et al would be jealous.

This disposition was mimicked by many of the religious. It was also copied by many that had apostolates to teach and train in seminaries. This was banned in the 1917 Code of Canon Law. It was, however, revived by the Legion of Christ, but they were told to stop after being discovered. The effects of these ideas of obedience were lessened by clear and unambiguous Canon Law, liturgical law, discipline, and very well-crafted rules for religious institutes that worked as a bulwark against the worst excesses of this tyrannical model. That is until Vatican II, when we will see what happens when the hounds are let loose.

In this context it is no wonder that the laity could only do what they were told, as they were most often treated as little children. But blind obedience by the laity led to a separation of religious belief and practice from the other adult areas of life, contributing to the secularization of western civilization. Because a layman is not formed in his beliefs into a mature and integrated believer, he either leaves the Faith, or has a separation of it in his life. In the one area he believes just as he did as a high-schooler, in the other he may be a very smart and successful, mature man. This separation within him, over time, becomes a separation in society, that of lived faith and blind obedience.

This totalitarian obedience in the hierarchy led to a totalitarian obedience in the various kingdoms of Europe. Reactions to these modes of governance would not take long, and they would have disastrous effects for both the rulers and the ruled, coming to full fruition in the "War to end all Wars".

Let us now turn back to the so-called "New World". Our Lord, Who is all-knowing and Who is working to save our souls, sent His very Mother yet again to us to call us to conversion and to warn us of the dangers that lay ahead. In the next chapter, we will look at another apparition of Our Lady, this time in Ecuador.

Chapter 2
Our Lady of Good Success of the Purification, 1594-1634

In this chapter, I give you a small collection of the statements of Our Lady. At the end of the chapter I will note a few things about this apparition and its historic framework. Our Lady of Good Success of the Purification appeared to Mother Mariana of Jesus Torres y Berriochoa, a nun of the Conceptionist Order, in Quito, Ecuador, from 1594-1634.

Prophecies of Our Lady of Good Success[ii]

During the 15th and 16th centuries, Our Lady of Good Success appeared in Quito, Ecuador, to a Spanish nun whose little-known but extraordinary life has a direct connection with our days. Our Lady told her that the pope's "infallibility will be declared a dogma of Faith by the same Pope chosen to proclaim the dogma of the mystery of my Immaculate Conception. He will be persecuted and imprisoned in the Vatican through the usurpation of the Pontifical States and through the malice, envy, and avarice of an earthly monarch."

"The same will occur with Holy Communion. Oh, how it hurts me to tell you that there will be many and enormous public and hidden sacrileges!" "In those times, the sacrament of Extreme Unction will be largely ignored.... Many will die without receiving it, being thereby deprived of innumerable graces, consolation, and strength in the great leap from time to eternity."

"The sacrament of Matrimony, which symbolizes the union of Christ with the Church, will be thoroughly attacked and profaned. Masonry, then reigning, will implement iniquitous laws aimed at extinguishing this sacrament. They will make it easy for all to live in sin, thus multiplying the birth of illegitimate children without the Church's blessing.... Secular education will contribute to a scarcity of priestly and religious vocations." "The holy sacrament of Holy Orders will be ridiculed, oppressed, and despised, for in this both the Church and God Himself are oppressed and reviled, since He is represented by His priests." "The devil will work to persecute the ministers of the Lord in every way, working with baneful cunning to destroy the spirit of their vocation and corrupting many. Those who will thus scandalize the Christian flock will bring upon all priests the hatred of bad Christians and the enemies of the One, Holy, Roman Catholic, and Apostolic Church. This apparent triumph of Satan will cause enormous suffering to the good pastors of the Church... and to the Supreme Pastor and Vicar of Christ on Earth who, a prisoner in the Vatican, will shed secret and bitter tears in the presence of God Our Lord, asking for light, sanctity, and perfection for all the clergy of the world, to whom he is King and Father.

"Unhappy times will come wherein those who should fearlessly defend the rights of the Church will instead, blinded despite the light, give their hand to the Church's enemies and do their bidding. But when [evil] seems triumphant and when authority abuses its power, committing all manner of injustice and oppressing the weak, their ruin shall be near. They will fall and crash to the ground.

"Then will the Church, joyful and triumphant like a young girl, reawaken and be comfortably cradled in the arms of my most dear and elect son of those times. If he lends an ear to the inspirations of grace— one of which will be the reading of these great mercies that my Son and I have had toward you— we shall fill him with graces and very special gifts and will make him great on Earth and much greater in Heaven. There we have reserved a precious seat for him because, heedless of men, he will have fought for truth and ceaselessly defended the rights of the Church, deserving to be called 'martyr.'

"At the end of the nineteenth century and throughout a great part of the twentieth, many heresies will be propagated in these lands...."'"The small number of souls who will secretly safeguard the treasure of Faith and virtues will suffer a cruel, unspeakable, and long martyrdom. Many will descend to their graves through the violence of suffering and will be counted among the martyrs who sacrificed themselves for the country and the Church."

Devotion to the Heart of Mary Will Save the World

"To be delivered from the slavery of these heresies, those whom the merciful love of my Son has destined for this restoration will need great will-power, perseverance, courage, and confidence in God. To try the faith and trust of these just ones, there will be times when all will seem lost and paralyzed. It will then be the happy beginning of the complete restoration...."

"In those times the atmosphere will be saturated with the spirit of impurity which, like a filthy sea, will engulf the streets and public places with incredible license.... Innocence will scarcely be found in children, or modesty in women." "He who should speak seasonably will remain silent."

"There shall be scarcely any virgin souls in the world. The delicate flower of virginity will seek refuge in the cloisters.... Without virginity, fire from heaven will be needed to purify these lands...." "Sects, having permeated all social classes, will find ways of introducing themselves into the very heart of homes to corrupt the innocence of children. The children's hearts will be dainty morsels to regale the devil...."

"Religious communities will remain to sustain the Church and work with courage for the salvation of souls.... The secular clergy will fall far short of what is expected of them because they will not pursue their sacred duty. Losing the divine compass, they will stray from the way of priestly ministry mapped out for them by God and will become devoted to money, seeking it too earnestly."

"Pray constantly, implore tirelessly, and weep bitter tears in the seclusion of your heart, beseeching the Eucharistic Heart of My Most Holy Son to take pity on His ministers and to end as soon as possible these unhappy times by sending to His Church the Prelate who shall restore the spirit of her priests."

Five Prophecies for Our Times

The most important of the apparitions of Our Lady of Good Success took place near the end of Mother Mariana's life. The early morning of February 2, 1634, the Feast of the Purification of the Blessed Virgin Mary, found Mother Mariana praying before the Blessed Sacrament, beseeching Him that she might be united with Him and be engulfed in that love which belongs to the Blessed. She also reminded Him to protect and preserve His daughters in that beloved Convent.

As she finished this prayer, she saw the sanctuary light extinguish itself, leaving the altar completely dark. Our Lady appeared to tell her that Our Lord had heard her clamors and would end her earthly exile in less than a year: "Prepare your soul so that, increasingly purified, it might enter into the fullness of the joy of Our Lord. Oh! If mortals, and, in particular, religious souls, could know what Heaven is and what it is to possess God! How differently they would live! Nor would they spare themselves any sacrifice in order to possess Him!"

The Blessed Virgin Mary then explained the five meanings of the Tabernacle light that had been extinguished before Mother Mariana's eyes.

First Prophecy

"The first significance is that at the end of the 19th century and into the 20th century, various heresies will be propagated in this land, then a free Republic. As these heresies spread and dominate, the precious light of Faith will be extinguished in souls by the almost total corruption of customs [morals]. During this period, there will be great physical and moral calamities, both public and private.

"The small number of souls who, hidden, will preserve the treasure of the Faith and the virtues will suffer an unspeakably cruel and prolonged martyrdom. Many of them will succumb to death from the violence of their sufferings, and those who sacrifice themselves for Church and Country will be counted as martyrs.""In order to free men from bondage to these heresies, those whom the merciful love of My Most Holy Son will destine for that restoration will need great strength of will, constancy, valor, and much confidence in God. To test this faith and confidence of the just, there will be occasions when everything will seem to be lost and paralyzed. This, then, will be the happy beginning of the complete restoration."

These chosen souls, who will restore the health of the Church, are described in detail as the apostles of the latter times, by St. Louis Marie de Montfort in his True Devotion to the Blessed Virgin Mary.

The Second Prophecy

"The second meaning," Our Lady said, "is that My Convent, being greatly reduced in size, will be submerged in a fathomless ocean of indescribable bitterness, and will seem to be drowning in these diverse waters of tribulations." Many authentic vocations will perish, She continued. Injustice would enter even this Convent, "disguised under the name of false charity, wreaking havoc in souls." And faithful souls, weeping in secret and imploring that such dire times be shortened, would suffer a continuous and slow martyrdom.

The Third Prophecy

"The third reason the lamp was extinguished is because of the spirit of impurity that will saturate the atmosphere in those times. Like a filthy ocean, it will run through the streets, squares and public places with an astonishing liberty. There will be almost no virgin souls in the world," Our Lady told her. The delicate flower of virginity would be threatened by complete annihilation. However, She promised that there would always be some good souls in cloisters where it might take root, grow, and live like a shield to deflect Divine Wrath. "Without virginity," She said, "it would be necessary for fire from Heaven to fall upon these lands to purify them."

The Fourth Prophecy

The fourth reason for the lamp being quenched is that the Masonic sects, having infiltrated all the social classes, would subtly introduce its teaching into domestic ambiences in order to corrupt the children, and the devil would glory in dining upon the exquisite delicacy of the hearts of children. "During these unfortunate times," Our Lady foretold, "evil will assault childhood innocence. In this way, vocations to the priesthood will be lost, which will be a true calamity." Again Our Lady promised that during this time there would still be religious communities who will sustain the Church and holy ministers of the altar— hidden and beautiful souls— who will labor with valor and disinterested zeal for the salvation of souls. "Against them," She warned, "the impious will rage a cruel war, letting fall on them vituperations, calumnies, and vexations in order to impede the fulfillment of their ministry. But they, like firm columns, will remain unswerving and will confront everything with the spirit of humility and sacrifice with which they will be vested, by virtue of the infinite merits of

My Most Holy Son, Who will love them in the innermost fibers of His Most Holy and Tender Heart."

During this time, Our Lady foretold, "the secular clergy will be far removed from its ideal, because the priests will become careless in their sacred duties. Lacking the Divine compass, they will stray from the road traced by God for the priestly ministry and they will become attached to wealth and riches, which they will unduly strive to obtain.

"How the Church will suffer on that occasion—the dark night of the lack of a Prelate and Father to watch over them with paternal love, gentleness, strength, discernment and prudence. Many priests will lose their spirit, placing their souls in great danger."

Our Lady continued to explain the fourth reason for the extinguishing of the Tabernacle light: "Therefore, pray insistently without tiring and weep with bitter tears in the secrecy of your heart. Implore our Celestial Father that, for the love of the Eucharistic Heart of My Most Holy Son and His Precious Blood shed with such generosity... He might take pity on His ministers and bring to an end those ominous times, and send to the Church the Prelate who will restore the spirit of Her priests." "My Most Holy Son and I will love this favored Son with a love of predilection, and We will gift Him with a rare capacity, humility of heart, docility to Divine inspiration, the strength to defend the rights of the Church, and a tender and compassionate heart, so that, like another Christ, He will assist the great and small, without despising the more unfortunate souls who ask Him for light and counsel in their doubts and hardships. Into His hands the scales of the Sanctuary will be placed, so that everything is weighed with due measure, and God will be glorified."

Our Lady continued, "The lukewarmness of all the souls consecrated to God in the priestly and religious state will delay the coming of this Prelate and Father. This, then, will be the cause of the cursed devil taking possession of this land, where he will achieve his victories by means of a foreign and faithless people, so numerous that, like a black cloud, it will obscure the pure heavens of the then Republic consecrated to the Sacred Heart of My Divine Son.

"With these people, all the vices will enter, which will attract in their turn every type of chastisement, such as plagues, famines, internal fighting and external disputes with other nations, and apostasy, the cause of the perdition of so many souls so dear to

Jesus Christ and to Me." "In order to dissipate this black cloud which prevents the Church from enjoying the clear day of liberty, there will be a formidable and frightful war, which will see the bloodshed of countrymen and foreigners, of secular and regular priests, and of religious. That night will be most horrible, for, humanly speaking, evil will seem to triumph.

"This, then, will mark the arrival of My hour, when I, in a marvelous way, will dethrone the proud and cursed Satan, trampling him under My feet and fettering him in the infernal abyss. Thus the Church and Country will finally be free of his cruel tyranny."

The Fifth Prophecy

The fifth reason that the lamp was extinguished is due to the laxity and the negligence of those who possess great wealth, who will indifferently stand by and watch the Church being oppressed, virtue being persecuted, and the triumph of the Devil, without piously employing their riches for the destruction of this evil and the restoration of the Faith. And it is also due to the indifference of the people in allowing the Name of God to be gradually extinguished and in adhering to the spirit of evil, freely delivering themselves over to vices and passions. "Alas! My chosen daughter! If it were given to you to live in that tenebrous era, you would die of sorrow to see all that I have revealed to you here take place. But My Most Holy Son and I have such a great love for this land, Our legacy, that We desire even now the application of your sacrifices and prayers to shorten the duration of such a terrible catastrophe!"

After the Prophecies

Overwhelmed by the magnitude of the evils she saw and the countless souls that would be condemned during these times, Mother Mariana fell unconscious. There the Sisters found her, as if dead, except for the violent beating of her heart. All of the doctor's efforts to restore her to consciousness proved useless. In fact he said, humanly speaking, her life should have ended from the shock she had received.

The Sisters surrounded her, beseeching Heaven to leave them their great treasure, the last of the Founding Mothers, "the mainstay of observance, the column of the house." Two days later, Mother

Mariana opened her eyes, encouraged her Sisters to continue to follow the Rule, and consoled them that she would remain with them yet a little longer.

Commentary

I would like to note a few things that have already happened, some that are happening now, and a few that certainly have not happened yet. First it was told that the pope would declare the dogmas of Papal Infallibility and the Immaculate Conception, all done. Next was a warning of the Masonic sect that would be reigning and working to destroy marriage, and, through secular education, to destroy vocations and corrupt the minds of the youth. This is happening now. There will be a lack of modesty and almost no virgin souls, which will require a purification of the world. The lack of modesty is obvious, but the purification by fire from heaven has clearly not happened, nor the smashing of the head of Satan and the full restoration of the Church. The spread of heresy everywhere is still going on, thanks to Modernism. One last note: She talks about the Masons nearly 100 years before they were founded in 1717 AD.

NB- She is called Our Lady of Good Success of the Purification for at least two reasons. First is that the apparition of the light being extinguished happened on that feast day. Second, is that the Purification of the world has not yet happened, and we should pray for the good success of this needed cleansing from, by, and through, Our Queen.

Chapter 3
How did we get here? Part Two
From the Peace of Westphalia to the Bloody Revolution

In this chapter we will look at the further splintering of Christendom, at how the heresy of Protestantism led to what was arguably the worst war to ever be waged in Europe, at how a skeptic, unable to keep faith and reason together, decides to subordinate faith to his own mind, at the story of an Englishman who witnesses the death of a king and decides to protect the state from religion by keeping religion out of politics, and, finally, at the story of a king who is asked by the Lord to promote devotion to His Sacred Heart and ignores Him for 100 years before losing the crown and his head. Listen to Our Lady.

<u>The most awful war in the history of the German people</u>
The Peace of Westphalia was signed in 1648. This officially ended the 30 Years War which resulted from the heresy of Martin Luther.

Luther failed to understand that grace builds on nature, and, as man is ever more endowed with grace, he is perfected. Luther believed that man is evil and that grace only covers over man with no change in him. He also rejected the authority of the Church. The areas of the faith so dutifully preserved and handed down to him that he did not or could not understand, he cut away.

Luther's beliefs led to a massive seizure of religious properties and goods by local nobility, especially in the northern parts of the Holy Roman Empire. Once they stole Church property, they of course then had to rebel openly to be able to keep it. Thus the 30 Years War resulted from the desire on the protestant side to keep their loot and only later grew into a desire to not be forced underground with their heresies. The Catholic side was represented by the Hapsburg dynasty, and generally wanted a unity of faith and a just return of stolen lands and goods. I say "represented" because the Holy Roman Empire was a conglomeration of over 100 territories and fiefdoms which elected the Emperor.

In our secular time, full of the enthronement of a rabid individualism, it must be noted that these Christians lived with the idea that the most important thing in life was to get to heaven, and the worst thing was to be damned. Further, just as a baby cannot live alone, so, too, we need community, both to live and, more importantly, for salvation.

Peace came with the idea that the belief of the prince was to be the accepted belief of the people *cuius regio, eius religio* (whose realm, their religion). Here, too, we see secular authority put above Divine Faith. If the Catholic Faith is the One True Faith, how could a Catholic affirm this legal principle? Perhaps it was a real world application of the nominalists.

This legal innovation required that those princes which had stolen from the Church remain outside the Church or lose their loot. Westphalia also resulted in the weakening of the Holy Roman Empire and the beginning of replacing Christ the King with a secular ruler in formerly Catholic Europe. Finally, because of the weakness of the Holy Roman Empire, a traditional defender of the Papal States, it was now only a matter of time before the pope would lose the Papal States. Thus, at least the appearance of removing the Kingship of Christ, the actual origin of all authority, had begun Christendom's march toward secularism. I say "appearance" because the Lord is King no matter if He is recognized as such or not.

Some historians, ever trying to explain the results of history, have noted that the rise of Protestantism resulted in the rise of "religious wars", and the 30 Years War was only the first and most terrible. NB- It took over sixty years, three generations, to bring the population of central Europe back up to pre-war times.

However, while it is true that the protestants and Catholics certainly fought over these coming centuries, before, when all were Catholic, there was still continual war throughout Europe. Despite that, the fantasy of making these same polities completely secular in the late 19th and early 20th centuries has led to now two of the most devastating wars the world has ever seen. The painful point is this: fallen men are ever inventive to find new reasons to go to war, kill their neighbor, and steal their lands and goods, regardless of innovation and "enlightenment".

I think, therefore... I don't know

René Descartes (1596- 1650), the father of Rationalism, trained by the Jesuits, became a skeptic and tried to use mathematical problem-solving to free himself from skepticism. On Nov. 10, 1619, he had a preternatural event that "opened" to him knowledge of all the sciences by a spirit entering into him. Catholics teach three realms in the universe: Natural, that which one can see, touch, smell, etc.; Preternatural, our souls, as well as angels and fallen angels; Supernatural, the domain of the Divine.

Still a skeptic, Descartes searched for truth and concluded, "I think therefore I am". This is a totally self-reflective statement. That is, he questions everything which he does not personally know or understand. He goes further to question anything outside of himself; he is always "perceiving" this or that to be true, but is it? He went on to say he rejected "all such merely probable knowledge and make it a rule to trust only what is completely known and incapable of being doubted". Thus Rationalism says, "There cannot be anything which exceeds the power of human reason to comprehend." The vast areas of the Faith are by default suppressed as they deal with mysteries that are beyond man's full comprehension in this life. This is the beginning of the separation of faith and reason in the modern world.

Faith is reduced to personal piety and emotion. In *Fides et Ratio, par 45,* John Paul II reflected, "As a result of the exaggerated rationalism of certain thinkers… there emerged eventually a philosophy which was separate from and absolutely independent of the contents of faith… what for Patristic and Medieval thought was in both theory and practice profound unity… was destroyed." Descartes claimed that, because he had made this destruction and could explain everything with material explanations, miracles were impossible.

Pascal noted that Descartes cannot explain the absence of God without noting that the "finger of God" started it all. By this, Descartes could get around one of St. Thomas Aquinas's arguments for the existence of God, the "unmoved mover", the one who started it all, but he couldn't avoid some reference to God.

Here again we see that Divine Faith is placed below human reason. This Rationalism, that is the requirement that all thought and truth be measured by human reason, further leads to the denigration of faith bellow reason. A more popular term these days for this Rationalism is "Cartesian" thinking. "Cartesian" is a quick reference point that allows for a whole group of applications of this model in a variety of schools. As we will see, this basic principle will be developed and applied multifariously.

I'm afraid of religious zealots, so let's separate Church and State

John Locke (1632-1704) was an English philosopher and physician widely regarded as one of the most influential of Enlightenment thinkers and commonly known as the "Father of Liberalism". Considered one of the first of the British empiricists, following the tradition of Sir Francis Bacon, Locke is equally important to "social contract" theory. This is the idea that rights do not come from God, but rather that they are inherent in man, and man alone directly makes a contract with other men to give power to the government.

An intellectual rationale was gaining ground and acceptance for placing man's self-governance outside and separate from Divine Faith. John Locke's writings influenced Voltaire and Jean-Jacques Rousseau, of the Bloody Revolution infamy, as well as the American revolutionaries. His contributions to classical republicanism and liberal theory are reflected in the United States Declaration of Independence. During this time in English history, there was a struggle between the new Anglicans and the faithful Catholics. Catholic priests at this time were hunted down and often killed. Thus Locke was looking for a way out of this situation. NB-his idea to separate church and state is his biggest error. Locke knew English history. He could see the results of a king leaving the Church and killing dissidents followed by Catholics regaining power and killing dissidents. Some Catholics might have plotted to kill the king and parliament. The first king in English history to be killed was dispatched near his college while he was studying. It almost makes sense to think that maybe the way out of this cycle is to take faith out of the political process.

Locke's theory of mind is often cited as the origin of modern conceptions of identity and the self, figuring prominently in the work of later philosophers such as Jean-Jacques Rousseau, David Hume, and Immanuel Kant. Locke was the first to define the *self* through a continuity of consciousness. He postulated that, at birth, the mind was a blank slate, or *tabula rasa*. Contrary to Cartesian philosophy based on pre-existing concepts, he maintained that we are born without innate ideas and that knowledge is instead determined only by experience derived from sense perception, a concept now known as Empiricism. He thus furthered the Rationalism of Descartes and linked the "truth" to the senses. Does this sound a little like the idea that "science" is the only real way to know the truth? Here also we see the beginning of the Western notion of an "independent" man, free from any truth that is outside of him, free to do whatever he pleases.

I would guess that Locke would not easily agree with the modern notion of extreme individualism, for he did after all ground his political thought in natural law. However, his mistake was to take Divine Law and faith— here I mean Catholic Faith— out of the conversation of the proper governance of man. Look around today at the chaos because of this. Without governance based on more than only natural law with an anchor in Divine Faith still tied to a living and teaching faith (magisterium), society will find a dilemma without an answer. Without the guidance of supernatural Faith towards virtue, law devolves into a series of meaningless rules with no true goal. As the Lord said, "the rulers of the Gentiles have absolute power and lord it over them." Mt 20:25.

Devotion to the Sacred Heart? No I'd rather lose my head

St. Margaret Mary Alacoque (1646-1690) experienced visions of Jesus Christ for most of her life, but thought them a normal part of life, and continued to practice austerity. She entered the Visitation Convent at Paray-le-Monial in May 1671 to become a nun. These visions showed her the "form of the devotion, the chief features being reception of Holy Communion on the first Friday of each month, Eucharistic adoration during a 'Holy Hour' on Thursdays, and the celebration of the Feast of the Sacred Heart". The Lord Jesus requested His love be made evident through her.

On June 17, 1689 the Sacred Heart of Jesus manifested to Saint Margaret Mary Alacoque. His commands to the King of France, Louis XIV, were to consecrate France to the Sacred Heart, put an image of the Sacred Heart on the French flag, and build a chapel in honor of the Sacred Heart. If he did this, then France, at that time easily the richest, most powerful, and fully Catholic nation in the world, would be blessed even more. His Jesuit and noble advisors told him not to, just in case he did and things went badly, also suggesting not to take direction from a lowborn nun. They wondered why the Lord hadn't told the king directly. For 100 years *to the day* the Kings of France delayed and did not obey. The French Revolution started in 1789. On June 17, 1789 the King of France was stripped of his legislative authority by the upstart Third Estate, and four years later the soldiers of the French Revolution executed the King of France, Louis XVI, with a guillotine, as if he were a common criminal.

The Masonic ideas of fraternity, equality, and liberty had been unleashed onto the public, the Bloody Revolution was on, along with the reign of terror which resulted in the execution, or death in prison, of about 40,000 people (10,000 in Paris alone). The Jesuits that had improperly counseled the Kings of France to disregard this command of Christ the King were chastised. Starting in 1759, they were slowly kicked out of European countries, and in 1773, the Holy See ratified their suppression. Ironically, the only place they were welcome was in Russia, being ruled at that time by Catherine the Great. Only in 1814 did Pius VII restore them.

St. Margaret Mary Alacoque was officially canonized on May 13, 1920 by Pope Benedict XV and, in 1928, Pope Pius XI upheld the Church's position regarding the credibility behind her visions of Jesus Christ. He stated Jesus "manifested Himself" to Margaret, and the chief features of devotion to the Sacred Heart are "reception of Holy Communion on the first Friday of each month, Eucharistic adoration during a 'Holy Hour' on Thursdays, and the celebration of the Feast of the Sacred Heart". We can see here some of the prophesies of Our Lady of Good Success of the Purification starting to take place, namely the rise of the Masons, breakdown of the family with society, and persecution of the Church (30,000 priests were exiled from France).

It is good to note that this bloodbath and chaos, following the 100 years of disobedience to the Lord, was at the same time as the mislabeled "Enlightenment". I say mislabeled because we see in this time a limiting of intellectual and academic thought to fewer and fewer areas of study and, at the same time, a great deal of effort in the study of esoteric and fringe ideas. At this time began, along with other ridiculous "studies", the masonic fascination with alchemy, which is the nonsensical idea of changing coal into gold. This is noted by the popes at the time and has been repeated by Popes John Paul II and Benedict XVI, see above.

The rise of Deism is also seen at this time. Deism is a heresy which holds that God is no more than the supreme intelligence or craftsman who had set the machine which was the world to run according to its own natural and scientifically predictable laws. In other words, God created it and then left it. It is believed that most of our founding fathers were Deists, a heresy which became entrenched around the time of the American revolt against England.

In the next chapter we will look at the response from Heaven. We are given the Miraculous Medal by Our Lady, Who appears in La Salette and Lourdes. More and more, God shows His Mercy by sending Her more and more often, as history trends towards chaos.

Chapter 4

Miraculous Medal, 1830; Our Lady of La Salette[iii], 1846;
Our Lady of Lourdes[iv] 1858

In this chapter we examine three apparitions of Our Lady that occurred in the mid-19th century. At this time, Christendom was fully fractured by the protestants, heretical philosophers were becoming extremely influential, and the Church had largely failed to remedy the problems. In response, Our Lord sent Our Lady, who brought with Her the consolation of the Miraculous Medal, severe warnings, and promises. Would She be heeded?

The Medal of the Immaculate Conception

The Madonna of the Miraculous Medal (or Medal of Our Lady of Graces, or Medal of the Immaculate Conception) was an apparition that occurred on November 27th, 1830. She appeared to the future Saint Catherine Labouré, a young nun of the congregation of the daughters of Charity of Saint Vincent de Paul in Rue du Bac, n. 140, Paris. The most famous apparitions of Saint Catherine are the ones involving the Immaculate Virgin of the Miraculous Medal. They happened in July and November 1830 in the Novitiate Chapel. On July 18th 1830, she woken up at 11:30PM, because she heard someone calling her name, and saw a mysterious child in front of her bed, inviting her to get up. "The Virgin Mary is waiting for you," the child told her while emanating rays of light at each step. Catherine identified the child as her own guardian angel. He led her into the Chapel where Our Lady was waiting for her sitting on the right side of the altar. Catherine said: "Then, I flung myself close to her, falling on my knees on the sanctuary steps, my hands resting in her knees. The Most Holy Virgin told me how I should behave with my confessor and many other things."

When asked about the Virgin's appearance, Saint Catherine could hardly find the words: "She was average height and so beautiful that I cannot describe her. She was standing; her dress was sunrise-white silk and 'virgin style', that is, high-necked and with smooth sleeves. A white veil went down from her head to her feet. Her hair was divided, and she wore some kind of bonnet with a three centimeter-wide crochet on it, gently laid on her hair. Her face was quite visible; her feet were upon a globe, or better, a half-globe, or at least I saw half of it." The Saint said she had kneeled in front of Our Lady and rested her hands on her knees in reverence.

During the second apparition on November 27th, 1830, around 5:30PM, the Virgin entrusted Catherine with the forge of the Miraculous Medal. The Virgin said that the medal would be a sign of love, a pledge of protection, and a source of grace for those who would trust in it. The Virgin herself showed Catherine what the medal should look like. Catherine said that Our Lady's feet were upon a half-globe during the apparition, which symbolizes the Earth, and they were crushing a green and yellow snake's head. The Virgin's hands were adorned with rings and precious stones, which projected rays of light of different intensity and color, downwards. The Virgin explained to Catherine that those rays "symbolize the graces I shed upon those who ask for them".

Catherine saw some kind of oval frame appearing around Our Lady, and a writing from her right hand to her left hand, creating a semicircle of words written in gold: "O Mary, conceived without sin, pray for us who have recourse to Thee". That became the front image of the Miraculous Medal: the Virgin crushing the Snake's head, as fore-  warned by the Bible ("And I will put enmity between you and the woman […] she will crush your head, and you will strike his heel", Gen 3.15). Rays of light shoot out from her hands, symbols of the graces granted by God, and the invocation, "O Mary, conceived without sin, pray for us who have recourse to Thee", frames the whole picture. The apparition continued, and the mystic picture seemed to rotate in front of Catherine's eyes, showing her what the reverse side of the Medal should depict: "There was the letter M (first letter of the name Mary) topped by a cross with no crucifix and with the letter I (first letter of the name Iesus, Jesus) as base. Below there were two hearts, one surrounded by thorns (Jesus's heart), the other pierced by a sword (Mary's heart). Twelve stars surrounded the whole picture. Then everything dissolved, as something that is switched off, and I was left there, full of something I don't know, good feelings, joy, comfort."

The reverse side of the Miraculous Medal means this: the M for Mary supports the cross without crucifix. The monogram I for Jesus (Iesus) intersects the M and the Cross, and symbolizes the salvation brought by Jesus and Mary, the indissoluble relationship that ties Jesus and His Most Holy Mother, becoming a witness of the salvation of humankind carried out by her Son, Jesus, and making her a participant in Christ's sacrifice. The heart crowned with thorns is the Sacred Heart of Jesus, while the heart pierced by a sword is the Immaculate Heart of Mary. The twelve stars symbolize the twelve tribes of Israel and the twelve apostles. The Virgin herself is also called Star of the Sea in the prayer, *Ave Maris Stella*. This medal, suggested to Saint Catherine by the Virgin so that she could have it forged and distributed, is called the Miraculous Medal, referring to the many healings and conversions it caused.

In February 1832, Paris was devastated by a terrible cholera epidemic, which caused more than 20,000 deaths. The Daughters of Charity distributed the first 2000 medals, and right away, people were healed and converted, earning from the Parisians the title, "Miraculous".

On December 8, 1854, Pope Pius IX, in the bull *Ineffablis Deus*, proclaimed: We declare, pronounce and define that the doctrine which holds that the Blessed Virgin Mary, at the first instant of her conception, by a singular privilege and grace of the Omnipotent God, in virtue of the merits of Jesus Christ, the Savior of mankind, was preserved immaculate from all stain of original sin, has been revealed by God, and therefore should firmly and constantly be believed by all the faithful." This is the Immaculate Conception.

Pope Pius XII canonized Catherine Labouré in 1947.

Our Lady of La Salette 1846[v]

Abp. William B. Ullathorne wrote a short book called *The Holy Mountain of La Salette: A Pilgrimage of the Year 1854*. It is about the apparition of the Virgin Mary witnessed by Maximin Giraud and Melanie Calvat at La Salette on September 19, 1846.

There is also a tract written by Melanie and published in 1879 called *The Apparition of the Blessed Virgin on the Mountain of La Salette*, bearing the imprimatur of Bishop Zola of Lecceby. Few copies of the 1879 tract were circulated, and it was published again more widely in 1904. A third printing in 1922, with a new imprimatur, finally resulted in Rome's placing of the tract on the Index of Prohibited Books in 1923. The decree of the Holy Office reads:

DAMNATUR OPUSCULUM: "L'APPARITION DE LA TRÉS SAINTE VIERGE DE LA SALETTE"

DECRETUM

Feria IV, die 9 maii 1923

In generali consessu Supremae Sacrae Congregationis S. Officii Emi ac Rmi Domini Cardinales fidei et moribus tutandis praepositi proscripserunt atque damnaverunt opusculum: *L'apparition de la trés Sainte Vierge* sur la montague de la Salette le samedi septembre 1846. —Simple réimpression du texte intégral publié par Mélanie, etc. Societé Saint-Augustin, Paris-Rome-Bruges, 1922; Acta Apostolicae Sedis, pp.287-288.

This tract is the source of the notion that Rome will lose the faith and the clergy will become terrible, among other things. When La Salette is mentioned, many people immediately speak of this notion as the primary element. Others have written about this, but let us just look at what happened, and what Our Lady actually said.

Public Message
These words of the apparition of the beautiful, weeping lady were recorded by ecclesiastical officials in 1847. From the above mentioned book by the archbishop, it is literal transcript. This is Melanie's recital of the events, Maximin's is nearly identical: [The children are watching over cows, they take a nap, and then they see a bright light and find Our Lady sitting and crying with her elbows on her knees and hers hands over her face.]

"The Lady rose up and crossed her arms and said to us. 'Come near, my children, be not afraid; I am here to tell you great news'... She said to us weeping, 'If my people will not submit, I shall be forced to let fall the hand of my Son. It is so strong, so heavy, that I can no longer withhold it. For how long a time do I suffer for you! If I would not have my Son abandon you, I am compelled to pray to him without ceasing; and as to you, you take no heed of it. However much you pray, however much you do, you will never recompense the pains I have taken for you.

"'Six days I have given you to labor, the seventh I had kept for myself; and they will not give it to me. It is this which makes the hand of my Son so heavy. Those who drive the carts cannot swear without introducing the name of my Son. These are the two things which make the hand of my Son so heavy.

"'If the harvest is spoilt, it is all on your account. I gave you warning last year in the potatoes but you did not heed it. On the contrary, when you found the potatoes spoilt, you swore, you took the name of my Son in vain. They will continue to decay, so that by Christmas there will be none left.'

"And as I did not well understand what was meant by potatoes (pommes de terre), I was going to ask Maximin what was meant by potatoes, and the Lady said to us:

'Ah! my children, do you not understand: I will say it in a different way.' Then she continued: [Melanie continues the recital in the patois of the country.]

'If the potatoes (las truffas) are spoilt it is all on your account. I gave you warning last, but you would not take heed of it. On the contrary, when you found the potatoes spoilt, you swore, and introduced in your oaths the name of my Son. They will continue to decay, so that by Christmas there will be none left. If you have corn it is no good to sow it; all that you sow the beasts will eat. What comes up will fall into dust when you thrash it. There will come a great famine. Before the famine comes, the children under seven years of age will be seized with trembling and will die in the hands of those who hold them; the others will do penance by the famine. The walnuts will become bad, and the grapes will rot. If they are converted, the stones and rocks will change into heaps of corn, and the potatoes will be self-sown in the lands.

44

[It is at this point that Our Lady tells the children, individually, secrets and forbidding them to tell anyone]

"'Do you say your prayers well, my children?' Both of us answered, 'Not very well, Madam.'

"'You must be sure to say them well, morning and evening. When you cannot do better, say at least an Our Father and a Hail Mary. But when you have time, say more.

"'There are none [who] go to Mass except a few aged women, the rest work on Sunday all the summer; and in the winter, when they know not what to do, the boys go to Mass only to mock at religion. During Lent, they go to shambles like dogs. Have you never seen corn that is spoilt, my children?'

"Maximin replied: 'No, Madam,' For me, I did not know which of us she asked this question; and I replied very gently: 'No, Madam, I have never seen any yet.'

"'You must surely have seen it, you my child, [turning to Maximin], once when you were near the farm of Coin, with your father. The master of the field told your father to go and see his ruined wheat. You went both together. You took two or three of the ears into your hands and rubbed them, and they fell all into dust; and then you returned home. When you were still half an hour's distance from Corps, your father gave you a piece of bread and said to you: 'Here, my child, eat some bread this year at least; I don't know who will eat any next year, if the corn goes on like that.'

"Maximin replied, 'Oh yes, Madam, I remember now; just this moment I did not remember.'

"After this the Lady, said to us in French, 'Well, my children, you will make this known to all my people.' She passed a little stream and turned again to us to say, 'Well, my children you will make this to be known to all my people.'"

Secret of Maximin

The authentic "secrets" to Maximin and Melanie were recovered from the Vatican archives in 1999: [René Laurentin, Michel Corteville, _Découverte du secret de la Salette_, 2002.]

"On September 19, 1846, we saw a beautiful Lady. We never said that this lady was the Blessed Virgin but we always said that it was a beautiful Lady. I do not know if it is the Blessed Virgin or another person. As for me, I believe today that it is the Blessed Virgin.

"Here is what this Lady said to me:'"If my people continue, what I will say to you will arrive earlier, if it changes a little, it will be a little later.

'"France has corrupted the universe, one day it will be punished. The faith will die out in France: three quarters of France will not practice religion anymore, or almost no more, the other part will practice it without really practicing it. Then, after [that], nations will convert, the faith will be rekindled everywhere.

"'A great country in the north of Europe, now Protestant, will be converted; by the support of this country all the other nations of the world will be converted.

"'Before all that arrives, great disorders will arrive, in the Church, and everywhere. Then, after [that], our Holy Father the Pope will be persecuted. His successor will be a pontiff that nobody expects.

"'Then, after [that], a great peace will come, but it will not last a long time. A monster will come to disturb it. All that I tell you here will arrive in the other century, at the latest in the year two thousand.'

Maximin Giraud July 3, 1851

Secret of Melanie

"'Mélanie, I will say something to you which you will not say to anybody:

'"The time of God's wrath has arrived!

"'If, when you say to the people what I have said to you so far, and what I will still ask you to say, if, after that, they do not convert, (if they do not do penance, and they do not cease working on Sunday, and if they continue to blaspheme the Holy Name of God), in a word, if the face of the earth does not change, God will be avenged against the people ungrateful and slave of the demon.

"'My Son will make his power manifest! Paris, this city soiled by all kinds of crimes, will perish infallibly. Marseilles will be destroyed in a little time. When these things arrive, the disorder will be complete on the earth, the world will be given up to its impious passions.

"'The pope will be persecuted from all sides, they will shoot at him, they will want to put him to death, but no one will be able to do it, the Vicar of God will triumph again this time. The priests and the Sisters, and the true servants of my Son will be persecuted, and several will die for the faith of Jesus Christ. A famine will reign at the same time.

"'After all these will have arrived, many will recognize the hand of God on them, they will convert, and do penance for their sins.

"'A great king will go up on the throne, and will reign a few years. Religion will re-flourish and spread all over the world, and there will be a great abundance, the world, glad not to be lacking nothing, will fall again in its disorders, will give up God, and will be prone to its criminal passions. [Among] God's ministers, and the Spouses of Jesus Christ, there will be some who will go astray, and that will be the most terrible.

"'Lastly, hell will reign on earth. It will be then that the Antichrist will be born of a Sister, but woe to her! Many will believe in him, because he will claim to have come from heaven, woe to those who will believe in him! That time is not far away, twice 50 years will not go by.

"'My child, you will not say what I have just said to you. (You will not say it to anybody, you will not say if you must say it one day, you will not say what that it concerns), finally you will say nothing anymore until I tell you to say it!'

"I pray to Our Holy Father the Pope to give me his holy blessing."

Mélanie Mathieu, Shepherdess of La Salette, Grenoble, July 6, 1851.

J.M.J.+

Commentary
The children of La Salette adamantly refused to disclose the "secret" messages, until finally, in 1851, they were persuaded to write the secrets and send them to the pope for his eyes only. It must be remembered that these prophesies are conditional. The condition is that people continue to offend God by not keeping the Sabbath holy, blaspheming against the Holy Name, and taking oaths in the name of God. The threatened famine happened in Ireland and Europe from 1845-1852, the apparition of La Salette

became the occasion of a great movement in popular Catholic devotion, assisted by the endorsement of the *Curé d'Ars* and Pope Pius IX, and so mitigated the deaths. This Catholic revival would be eclipsed by the even greater pilgrimages to Lourdes after the apparitions of Our Lady there in 1858.

France has corrupted the world, the errors of France led to the errors of the communists in Russia, and the errors in Russia have now spread through the entire world. The Masonic revolution, under the titles of secularism and liberalism, is the seedbed of the horrors witnessed in the 20th century until today. Trying to put all this into a timeline, we can see first that the Pope, who was Pius IX, was persecuted and became a prisoner in the Vatican, 1870. Cardinal de Angelis was the front-runner to follow him but died months before the Conclave that elected Leo XIII, 1878. Thus Leo XIII is the "unexpected one". The final triumph of the pope has not yet happened, since the Papal States are still occupied by a foreign power, but the popes of those times still held fast to the faith and proclaimed it to the world.

The apparition next warns of a war followed by peace and then another war. Now we know it was WW1 and WW2. Paris was mostly destroyed in the Franco-Prussian War forty years before WWI; Marseilles was largely destroyed by the Nazis in 1944. These were a chastisement that resulted from much of France losing the faith. The peace that came between the wars was broken by a monster. Some think the monster was Hitler, but I think this is too narrow: the monster was a rabid nationalism. This nationalism is a monster because it goes directly against the First Commandment to worship only God, instead leading men to worship the State. Thus we can see that this monster actually infected, to varying degrees, all of the major and some minor combatants in both of the world wars on all sides.

The great king that came is probably Charles de Gaulle, President 1959-69, who was a practicing Catholic and was reviled by the leftists in France. There was a general revival of faith in Europe and the world, outside of the communist-controlled lands, after WW2. However, as prosperity returned, so, too, did a lack of faith and a rise in decadence. At the same time we know of the modernist clerics that came to the fore and the number of "Spouses of Jesus Christ" (female religious) that both left the Church and corrupted Her. Indeed this is the worst and "most terrible". Sadly, however, a more severe chastisement for the Church was yet to come.

Then we hear of an Antichrist that was supposed to come around not more than 100 years from the date of the apparition, thus by at least 1946. At minimum, then, he would be about 75 years old today if he had come. Instead, it is reasonable to say that this part of the prophesy has been deferred to a later time.

Finally, there is a promise that a protestant country from the north of Europe will be converted, and, by the support of this country, all the other nations of the world will be converted. Of course this has not happened. One example is the USA, not a Catholic country, let alone all the other heretical countries.

This last may have been a promise that if the people truly had done penance and prayed then England would have been converted and spread the true faith around the world. One can note men like St. John Henry Newman, G.K. Chesterton, Hilliare Bellock, and C.S. Lewis (who might have become Catholic) to name a few that give an idea of what that conversion would have looked like, but it is a bare glimmer of what would have happened, and the faith was only revived a small amount in England and Ireland. Neither other countries nor the world were converted. As we will see in the apparitions of Fatima, that mantle was passed on to Russia. We are still waiting for her conversion through Our Lady.

Our Lady of Lourdes 1858

First apparition

On February 11th, 1858, Bernadette Soubirous, 14 years old, while out collecting fire wood, was visited by Our Lady and prayed a rosary with her. That same evening while praying the family rosary, Bernadette broke out in tears, repeating her favorite invocation: "Oh, Mary, conceived without sin, pray for us who have recourse to thee."

Second apparition

On February 14th, everyone had thought that what happened to Bernadette was from the devil, and she was told to return to the grotto and pour holy water. When arriving at the Grotto, Bernadette asked the people to kneel and pray the holy rosary. The

Blessed Mother appeared again. Bernadette's face was transfigured. She sprinkled holy water and said: "If you come from God, come near us." The holy water touched the Blessed Mother's feet, and she came closer to Bernadette with a gentle smile. She took the holy rosary and made the sign of the cross. Both started to pray.

Third apparition

On February 18th, a lady and a religious accompanied Bernadette to the grotto. They went first to Mass with her at 5:30 am and from there to the grotto. Bernadette kneeled and started to pray the rosary. Then she screamed with joy to see Our Lady at the end of the grotto. She asked her if she may stay with her two companions, and the Blessed Mother agreed. They also kneeled, started to pray the rosary, and lit a blessed candle. Bernadette handed a paper to Our Blessed Mother and asked her to write down what she desired to communicate. The Virgin said: "What I have to communicate is not necessary to write down, just grant me the gift of coming here during 15 consecutive days." Bernadette promised Our Lady to do so and Our Lady responded: "I also promise to make you happy, not in this world, but in the next."

The fifteen miraculous days

February 19th: Bernadette arrived at the grotto accompanied by her parents and many people. From this day on she went to all the apparitions with a lighted candle

February 20th: about 500 people went with Bernadette.

February 21st: hundreds and thousands of people filled the grotto area. Bernadette approached on her knees. She observed that Our Blessed Mother became saddened. She asked her: "What is wrong? What can I do?" The Blessed Mother responded: "Pray for sinners."

February 22nd: The Blessed Mother did not appear. All the people made fun of Bernadette.

February 23rd: The first time the Blessed Virgin orders something concrete. Before 10 million people Our Blessed Mother gave Bernadette a secret that only she can keep and not give to anyone. She also taught her a prayer to repeat, but not to let others know it. The Blessed Mother said: "Now, my daughter, go and tell the priest to erect in this place a Sanctuary, and people should come here in procession."

Bernadette went immediately to the church to give the message to the Pastor. The priest asked her the name of the lady and Bernadette responded that she did not know it.

After listening to her, the pastor said: "Can you understand that your testimony alone is not enough for me. Tell the lady to let herself be known; if it is the Virgin, may she manifest it through a great miracle. Did you not tell me that she appears on a wild rose bush? Well then, tell the lady for me that if she wants a sanctuary, may the rose bush blossom."

February 24th: Bernadette as usual arrived at the grotto and kneeled without paying attention to the curiosity of the people around her. Bernadette told Mary what the priest requested. Our Blessed Mother only smiled without saying a word. She then asked her to pray for sinners and exclaimed three times: "Penance, Penance, Penance!" She asked Bernadette to repeat these words and she did so as she kneeled towards the back of the grotto. Mary revealed a personal secret there and then disappeared.

Because of her humility Bernadette did not relate all the details, but witnesses recount that they also saw her kiss the ground at different times. The Blessed Mother said to her: "Pray for sinners . . . you will kiss the ground for the conversion of sinners." As the vision moved back, Bernadette would follow it kneeling and kissing the ground. Bernadette turned to the people and said with signs: "You also kiss the ground."

Since then Bernadette received the mission to do penance for sinners. One day the Virgin asked her to go up and down the grotto on her knees. The Virgin's face was very sad. "The Virgin has ordered this for me and for others," Bernadette said.

February 25th: Mary said: "My daughter, I want to entrust the last secret only to you; just as the last two, do not reveal them to any person in this world."

After a moment of silence the Virgin said: "And now go and drink, and wash your feet at the fountain, and eat the grass there."

Bernadette looked around her and saw no fountain. She thought the Virgin was sending her to the stream nearby and ran to it. The Blessed Mother stopped her and said: "Don't go there, go to the fountain that is here." She pointed to the grotto.

Bernadette went up and stopped near the rock. She looked for the fountain with no success, and so as trying to obey, she looked at Mary. Having been given a new sign from Mary, Bernadette stooped down and started digging into the dirt with her hands, successfully digging a hole. All of a sudden, it started to become humid, and, coming from unknown depth, through the rocks, water started to appear and rapidly filled the hole with enough water to fill a glass.

Mixed with swampy dirt, Bernadette put it on her lips three times, with no intention of drinking it. Overcoming her repugnance to the dirty water, she drank it and wet her face. The people started to laugh and made fun of her, saying she was mad. But in God's mysterious designs, Bernadette with her fragile hands just unknowingly opened the spring of healings and great miracles that have moved humanity.

The miraculous water of Lourdes has been examined by prominent scientists: it is virgin water, very pure, natural water, lacking thermal properties. Also, it has the particularity that no bacteria live in this water (Symbol of the Immaculate Conception, in which there never was in her a stain of original or personal sin).

February 26th: The miraculous waters produced the first miracle. The good pastor of Lourdes had asked for a small sign, but the Blessed Virgin gave the entire population and him a very large one.

The first miracle of healing

In Lourdes lived a poor working man, a stone cutter named Bourriette who had his left eye mutilated by a mine explosion 20 years ago. He was a very honest and Christian man. He sent his daughter to the new fountain for water and started to pray. Even though the water was dirty he rubbed his eye with it. He then started to scream with joy. The darkness disappeared: nothing but a small cloud was left which also disappeared as he continued washing his eye with the water. Doctors had said that he would never recover his sight. Upon examining him again, no choice was left but to call it a miracle.

March 2nd: Bernadette goes again to see the pastor of Lourdes, reminding him of Mary's request to build a sanctuary on the sight of the apparitions. The pastor said it was a work for the

Bishop who is already aware of the petition and the one responsible to fulfill the celestial desire of the vision.

March 4th: On the last day, as was her usual habit, Bernadette went to Holy Mass before going to the grotto. At the end of the apparition she felt deep sadness, the sadness of separation. "Will I see the Virgin again?"The Virgin, always generous, did not allow the day to end without a manifestation of her goodness: a great miracle, a maternal miracle, the crowning of the fifteen apparitions.

The miracle: a two-year old child named Justino who was, at his young age, already in agony. Since birth he had a high fever that little by little was deteriorating his life. On the day of the miracle, his parents thought he was dead. The mother in desperation took the child and ran to the fountain. The child did not have any vital signs. The mother immersed the child in the cold water for 15 minutes. After she returned to the house, she noticed the child was breathing normally. The following day, Justino woke up with a healthy complexion, his eyes full of life, asking for food, and his legs strengthened. This event moved the whole region and soon afterwards all of France and Europe. Three well known doctors certified the miracle, naming it of first degree.

March 25th: Feast of the Annunciation, Bernadette asked Our Lady again: "In your kindness, can you please tell me who you are and what is your name ?" The vision was brighter than ever, always smiling, and her smile was the only response. Bernadette insisted: "Can you please tell me who you are? I beg you, my Lady."

Then the Lady's gaze left Bernadette and went heavenward. The Virgin separated her hands and slipped down her arm the rosary which she held on her fingers, raising at the same time her hands and her radiant head. Her hands united again in front of her chest and her gaze was more brilliant than the light, pointed at heaven, and she said: "I AM THE IMMACULATE CONCEPTION." She then disappeared, leaving Bernadette with this image and name.

Bernadette heard those words for the first time. While she headed to the rectory to tell the pastor (he had ordered her to ask the name of the vision), she repeated along the way "Immaculate Conception". They were mysterious and difficult words for an illiterate child.

Upon hearing the events from Bernadette, the pastor was astonished. How can a girl without any religious instruction know about a dogma only proclaimed by the Church four years ago? In 1854, Pope Pius IX had defined the dogma of the Immaculate Conception.

April 5th: Monday of Easter. Bernadette returned to the grotto, surrounded by a multitude of people praying with her. As usual she kneeled, and in her left hand she held the lighted candle that she always took with her. She placed it on the ground.

Absorbed in contemplation of the Queen of Heaven, more so now that she was assured of the identity of the Blessed Virgin Mary, Bernadette raised her hands and as she brought them down again she did not realize that she was touching the flame of the candle. The flame began to pass through her hand, penetrating her fingers from side to side, as wind gusted.

People started to scream: "She is getting burned." But she remained motionless. A doctor near Bernadette confirmed with his watch that for more than 15 minutes her hand was on the flame without moving whatsoever. Everyone screamed "miracle!" The doctor confirmed that Bernadette's hand was unharmed.

The last apparition

July 16th – Feast day of Our Lady of Mt. Carmel. Bernadette again felt urged to visit the grotto which was fenced, guarded, and prohibited. She was accompanied by her aunt and some neighbors and crossed through the grassland adjacent to the grotto. They knelt as close as possible to the grotto without actually arriving there. Bernadette received the last visit from the Blessed Mother and said: "she never appeared so glorious." Bernadette accomplished her mission with great love and courage among all the sufferings endured and obstacles by the enemy in her path. Her confessor said repeatedly: "The greatest proof of the apparitions is Bernadette herself, her life."

Summary of the Messages of the Virgin Mary of Lourdes

The messages the Blessed Virgin Mary gave at Lourdes, France in 1858 are summarized as follows:

1- It is an appreciation from heaven of the definition of the dogma of the Immaculate Conception, declared four years prior (in 1854). At the same time, she presents herself as Mother and model of purity for the world in need of this virtue.

2- It is an exaltation to the virtues of poverty and humility accepted in a Christian way by having chosen Bernadette as an instrument of her messages.

3-It is about the Cross. The Blessed Mother repeats that the most important thing is to be happy in the other life, even though it is necessary to accept the Cross to achieve happiness.

4- The importance of prayer, the rosary, penance, and humility (kissing the ground as a sign); a message of infinite mercy for sinners and for the care of the sick.

Important points for reflection about the visible signs in the first apparition which include great spiritual teachings:

1- Surrounded by light: this is a symbol of the light of faith which we receive at Baptism. Faith is the light of life with which we should shine before the world. We should transmit the brilliance of faith by our sanctity of life.

2- The light was tranquil and profound: in our Christian faith we find repose for our souls.

3- Incomparable beauty, there is nothing like it here on earth: work unceasingly to acquire true beauty of soul which God is pleased to contemplate.

4 - White dress, pure and delicate, never imitated: our soul should be dressed in purity and be delicate before God; sin stains our white dress.

5- Bare feet, on top of which is a brilliant rose: bare feet preach to us about the evangelical poverty of the Gospels which is a beautiful and sublime virtue. To those who practice it, Jesus has promised the Kingdom of Heaven.

The luminous rose is a call to be the fragrance of Christ to all, the divine fragrance of the Gospels.

6- Her hands always together, with the Holy Rosary in fervent prayer, praying always without ceasing: prayer is our constant nourishment, the breath of our soul, all the virtues are born in the soul that prays.

Our Lady of Lourdes, pray for us!

<u>The apparitions of Our Lady of Lourdes and the Church</u>

January 18th, 1862: the Bishop signed the pastoral letter approving the apparitions, its supernatural character, and the authentic life of the visionary.

1874: Pope Pius IX granted the sanctuary the title of Basilica.

1876: solemnly crowned the statue of the Virgin.

Leo XIII: approved the office of mass for Lourdes.

Pius X: named Lourdes the "Throne of power and mercy of Mary, where marvelous apparitions of Mary took place."

1907: this same Pope extended the celebration of the Feast Day of Lourdes to the universal Church.

Pius XI: affirmed: "Lourdes is the place where the Blessed Virgin appeared several times to the blessed Bernadette who exhorted all men to penance."
He elevated St. Bernadette Soubirous to the altar on December 8th, 1933.

Pius XII: wrote the encyclical "The pilgrimage to Lourdes," the most complete document on Lourdes.

John XXIII: in the closing of the centenary of the apparitions of Lourdes, he recalled the following, "The Church, through the voice of the Popes, does not cease in recommending to Catholics to pay attention to the messages of Lourdes."

Finally, John Paul II is the first pope to go on a pilgrimage to Lourdes in 1983, with the motive of the 125th anniversary of the apparitions. He celebrated Holy Mass on August 15th, affirming twice: "We come in pilgrimage to Lourdes, where Mary said to Bernadette: I'm the Immaculate Conception. Here she spoke to a simple girl of Lourdes, prayed with her the holy rosary, gave her several messages." The Pope concluded: "The Blessed Virgin comes to save sinners."

August 14th, 2008 the Holy Father returned to Lourdes to honor Mary on the 150th anniversary of the proclamation of her Immaculate Conception.

Throughout the Holy Father's two-day pilgrimage, he was absorbed in prayer as he visited the Sacred Grotto where Our Lady appeared, prayed with pilgrims, and celebrated Mass on the Feast of the Assumption. Speaking from the balcony of the Accueill Notre Dame Center on the eve of the Assumption, the Pope referred to Our Lady's apparitions to Bernadette as a "dialogue between Heaven and earth which has continued and which is still ongoing."

In the next chapter, we will look at how the world responded to Our Lady: the French Revolution, and the first absolute rejection of the Church in a Catholic country.

Chapter 5
How did we get here? Part Three
From Napoleon to Vatican I, 1868

In this chapter, we will pick up were we left off with the Bloody Revolution of France, starting with the philosophical underpinnings of true skepticism. The Napoleonic Wars at the end of the Bloody Revolution caused massive destruction in areas including physical and economic, and this led to the further weakening of the Church and State relationship. We will see that once objective truth is called into question, faith and reason become separated. The wars of the time destroyed much of the old order, and the lack of clear thinking led to a re-evaluation of fundamental questions: How did we get here? Where did we come from? What is the purpose of life? One man decides we must have come from slime or monkeys. We will see how the Church responded to these errors and tried to both protect the faith and spread the good news.

We don't know anything, so certainly I can't know God
Emmanuel Kant (1724-1804) took up the skepticism of Descartes and tried to answer the question of how we know things, epistemology. He claimed that it is not the mind and senses that are influenced by reality, but rather reality is influenced by the mind. The analogy he used was a stick in water. Take a stick and put it in water, and it looks like it is bent or broken at the water line. Remove the stick, and it's straight again. Thus, he concludes that the mind both bent or broke the stick and put it back together. He did not know the rules governing light and refraction. The stick was never broken or bent in reality.

Descartes's idea led to a further strengthening of the rationalist position which resulted in the final confrontation and defeat, at that time, of German philosophy which was trying to hold onto the link between faith and reason. Kant concluded that reason can only be limited to the natural, "lower" sciences, and faith is only an accent of the will with no "pure reason" for it. Thus the Cartesian principles are applied. Remember also the "enlightenment" wanted to only use part of the Aristotelian model of causality. Aristotelian Causality has four parts: 1. Formal; 2.

Material; 3. Efficient; 4. Final. The formal (what it is) and the final (what it is going to be) are blotted out. Only the material (what it is made of) and efficient (how it is made) will remain for Kant.

For practical purposes he invented a new morality that is based on the "categorical imperative". That is, based on "pure reason" without reference to anything outside of the mind. He concludes that our actions should be based on our duties or the law. Thus, we see the idea of legal Positivism, a new phrase that is really a tip of the cap to Nominalism. Kant successfully separated faith and reason in at least his own mind. But here we can see a very dangerous train of thought. If one separates the Four Causes taught by Aristotle and used by the Church, including especially the scholastics who have St. Thomas Aquinas as their pinnacle, what is left?

Without knowing what something actually is (first cause, formal) or the purpose that it serves, (fourth cause, final), everything is reduced to a function. In other words, all that remains is the question, out of what is it made and how is it it made? Everything and everyone is only given value based on the usefulness that it has. This results in judging everything and everyone on the totally subjective, self-centered notion of utility. People start making things and doing things while only asking the question of can we do this or that, and, never, should we? The "new morality" of Kant allows for this type of thinking and action. When there is no objective truth in reality, then reality is the myth. For example, today someone could say, " That chicken is acting like a hound dog; it must be a hound dog". Of course this is nonsense. There are men today that say, " I feel like I'm a woman; I must be a woman". Again, this is nonsense. If you say that the tail of a dog is a leg, how many legs does the dog have? Four: a tail cannot be a leg. But for the Kantian, it has five legs.

Imagine driving down a road only to find a large gate blocking the road. If it is taken down, some might look around and not realize the purpose for the gate, then simply drive past where it was, not knowing it was put there to stop people from driving past it. They quickly find the reason out when their vehicle becomes stuck in a sinkhole. A wiser man might say, "I'm not sure why this gate was here, but there must be a good reason," and turn back around.

The "categorical imperative" of Kant is that way of life and action which is based on law and duty without regard to a supernatural law. It has led to some of the worst tragedies in history. Why or in what way can a man or a group of men excuse the deaths of the last 100 years? The deaths in war are bad, but how about the deaths in internment camps? How about the billions of little babies slaughtered, still in the wombs of their mothers? How does a group of otherwise well-educated men think that making a bigger bomb is a great idea? Why not say no, I will not do that, or build this?

The little emperor and a new world order without God

It is kind of funny to think that the popular notion of Napoleon Bonaparte, the great and mighty warlord that conquered most of Europe, was that he was, in fact, a little fella. He was 5'6", so actually slightly above average height for his time and just about average height for our own time. The reason people think this is for two reasons. First, he really liked to have his closest lieutenants to be tall, the shortest over 6'4". Thus, the contrast made Napoleon seem shorter than he was. Second, those countries fighting against him learned of this and used it to make fun of him, especially the English. Why not? For many years he was nearly unbeatable on the battlefield. His enemies had to have some way to keep the morale of the troops up. Besides, everyone makes fun of their enemies.

From 1799-1814, Napoleon was the leader of the French. The last ten of those years he named himself emperor. The title was a change, but in reality, he was the total ruler for fifteen bloody years. We don't need to get into all the details of this time or how he made a short return to "rule" for about a month in 1815 only to die in exile in 1821 on the island of St. Helena under the watchful eyes of the English. Many have written of this time. I will focus on just a few things of note.

After the ten years of bloody revolution, 1789-1799, under the banner of "liberty, equality, fraternity", Napoleon was made "first consul". Five years later, he named himself emperor. While the reign of terror, started and inspired by the Masons, wanted to destroy everything that was Catholic, which is the good, the true, and the beautiful, they realized that it actually would not work out to kill each and every believer. There wouldn't be anyone left.

Enter Napoleon. He was a good military leader and politically astute enough to retain some of the old structures of society. It turns out that fallen man tends to be rather unruly without something beyond, or outside of himself, for which to live. The idea of a State was just not going to cut it. Napoleon did not have a problem working with the Church, so long, in his mind, as the Church knew from where the real power came. This is why, when he was to be crowned emperor, he insisted that the pope be there and do it, just as the popes had crowned emperors of the past, most notably Charlemagne. However at the moment the pope was to rise and place the crown on his head, Napoleon took it, crowning himself and his wife. Thus, he humiliated the pope and symbolically placed the Church as subordinate to the State.

It's true there is no reason for my faith, but it feels good

Friedrich Schleiermacher (1768-1834) is the father of Romanticism, a system that could not defend faith and reason working together. As the rationalist destroyed the Lutheran philosophers' reasons for faith, they were left with the question of explaining this faith. (Luther taught that faith and reason were separated, and Kant, a Lutheran, systemized this thought.) They concluded that they could not explain their faith. Faith for them is unreasonable, but it is not reason that makes it worthy of man, it is the experience that makes it have value. For some it is the "smells and bells", for others, it is a well crafted sermon, and for yet others, it is the architecture, art, and music. In any event, for those all that was left was the subjective experience. All they have is emotion and experience. For them, religion must spur on or inspire (manipulate) people's emotions, in order for it to be of value. The rise of the "mega-churches" with a concert-like atmosphere is the necessary conclusion. The rise of the famous television "preachers" with their cult of personality is the endpoint of this surrender.

The rationalist then moved on to their next conquest, but Romanticism lives on quite strongly today. Even in the Church. "It's all about the experience," many say. Some even within the Church try to mimic, rather poorly, the inane activities of the "mega-church". There are constant changes in these gatherings, because the need to feed people's emotions is never ending. With faith and reason separated, now the lower faculties (emotions) placed above the higher faculties (reason), the road to "man as a mere animal" is laid. Sadly, when the most important relationship for man, one with God, had been reduced to merely an experience, or rather the emotion that comes from the experience, this poison naturally spreads into other relationships.

Hence the rise of romance: novels, songs, musicals, movies, etc. This collection of works, this genre, has certainly spread throughout the world. It has become so pervasive that many people can't even think about their relationships outside of how it feels. This genre can be properly described as a woman's way of porn. Or simply, women's porn. This perverted way of looking at life has destroyed many marriages and other relationships. Observe that people who live their lives based on an emotional reaction will even leave their parish or the Church at large because they "aren't getting what they need (want)". How mindless have so many become to sit in judgment of the Holy Sacrifice of the Mass— which exists principally for the glory of God, praise and thanksgiving to Him— and then say, "I didn't get anything out of that."

It should not be lost that this way of women's porn spread far and was accepted widely, in large part, before real pornography, created for men, spread. It is a repeat of history: Eve sinned, then Adam followed. Note today, people are calling for the end of porn, the stuff directed at men, but do not call for the porn directed at women.

The Romance genre is porn for woman because it presents a fantasy. Women's relationships with the world are fantasized to varying degrees, sometimes emphasizing men (husband or lover), sometimes children, sometimes finances (money, houses, cars, etc.). Often, the really popular ones have aspects of all these things. But the core is a fantasy that these people and things all serve the woman to make her feel good, important, accepted, and loved for who she is with no need for her to change or do anything.

Women are more complicated than men. Porn for men is obvious, and it presents people, usually women, for the physical gratification of men. Again, women's porn gratifies the emotions of women, men's porn gratifies the physical, or at least that is what is sold. They both fail and destroy people because they are lies based in fantasy not reality.

Darwin and an explanation of origins, without God
Charles Darwin (1809-1882) wrote his *Origin of Species* in

1859, and it is considered the basis for evolutionary theory. This theory takes the rationalist philosophy and applies it to the philosophical question of origins which is fundamental to man: Where did we come from? These ideas are not exactly original to Darwin. In fact, it is written that another Englishman was finishing his own work on this idea, and Darwin found out about it and simply beat him to the press. In any event, the only "new" thing was that he used some biology to "prove" his theory. He knew, of course, that his book had major holes and hoped that the lack of evidence would be produced by later followers. He admitted that if they could not find the "missing link" the whole idea would fail. Since this has never been found, I guess if we are honest, the whole idea *has* failed.

Darwin posited that there is a mechanism in nature that directs the advancement of organism from simple to more complex. The heart of this theory is based on the hypothesis that things which direct the operation of cells change themselves over time into more complex organisms. This is supposed to be a random series of events that require millions of years.

The central idea of random mutations over time resulting in a string of better and more advanced species is nonsense. The second law of thermodynamics, entropy, states that an isolated system tends to deteriorate over time, not become more sophisticated or complex. If the mechanism to do this worked, it would require trillions of years to accomplish, not millions. He did not know cell biology, gene theory, or DNA as we do. But the millions of years proposed is mathematically impossible.

I wonder if, now that the theory requires trillions of years, carbon dating will suddenly change to fit the new math? Just as the dating of the "big bang" was given to fit the old math. Now that man is reduced to merely an animal, the rationalist had to come up with an origin story. As they were determined to undermine the Church, the story had to be one without God.

At the same time Ernst Haeckel was spreading the rationalist/materialist ideology into German "lower" scientific thought. Darwin's book came at a perfect time to expand this movement even further. These groups were often called naturalists and included men of cosmology and medicine.

Frederick Nietszche was also writing at this time, and you could say he finished the thoughts of Descartes and Kant. He concluded that while we cannot know anything objectively, and because we can and do control our own reality, the way forward, the only thing left, is for each individual to go beyond our nature as it is and to become "supermen". These "supermen" would be guided only by the will, a will directed to power. He finishes this thought to its logical end which is nihilism, utter ruin and nothingness. He died probably the only true atheist ever, having lost his mind.

The philosophy of the materialist rationalist was now complete. It caused the utter suicide of rational thought. Having "proved" that we cannot know anything outside ourselves, the only thing left is brute conquest and a license to pursue anything that will bring an emotional euphoria, even if it only lasts a few moments. As God, the eternal Good and the source of lasting joy, has been discarded, now only the animal, man, is left to do as he wills.

To this end, one might wonder as to some of the results of this "modern" way of thinking. Notice that it is not until the "modern" times that drug and rampant alcohol abuse are part of society. Of course people have always had too much to drink from the time of Noah, but drug abuse only became known in the recent centuries, and it did not spread into large parts of society until the "Opium Wars". That history is for another book.

These are errors of our time, you have been warned... thrice

The First Vatican Council ended in 1868 and was important for two reasons: it confirmed Papal Infallibility and explained it; and it defined the Immaculate Conception (fulfilling the prophesy by Our Lady in chapter two). Around that time and afterwards, the popes were responding to the heretical and dangerous developments in human thought in Christendom.

Pope Pius IX in 1864 wrote, *The Syllabus of Errors*, against Pantheism, Naturalism, absolute Rationalism, moderate Rationalism, and more that had crept into the theology of the Church. The so-called "higher criticism" of the time had lost its way. Those academics who where commenting on the Sacred Texts were being lead to erroneous conclusions due to an uncritical usage of some of the new techniques of literary study. Pius IX addressed these errors and warned of a slavish adherence to the above mentioned ideas. A cadre of Englishmen held fast to a rigid defense of Rationalism with a new emphasis on Darwin's thesis. Pius IX's list called out "the new Englishmen", who in turn in 1865 started a new publication *Nature* that would give them a place to spread their errors. These men were able to systematically take over the English academic community, and by the early 20th century, they took over the American National Academy of Science as well.

Pope Leo XIII wrote *Provindentissimus Deus* in 1893 to continue to combat the rationalists that denied the Divine Revelation, Inspiration, and Inerrancy of Sacred Scripture. He warned that the rationalist, in these denials, could weaken the belief of Catholics and the youth. If they believed these arguments against the Sacred Texts on even a few points, they could then easily be led to moral errors. His correction was to have the teachers of Sacred Scripture hold an understanding of the Natural Sciences with which to detect errors and defend their students. Sadly, most teachers of the time, and today, accept uncritically the claims of the rationalists, not realizing that these very claims are meant to undermine the faith, not to put forward reasonable scientific hypotheses. Leo XIII hoped that learned men of reputation would defend the Catholic position of a unity of faith and reason, and thereby silence those that claim that faith is the enemy of science. Here, too, most people today think there is no connection between faith and reason.

The Pope could see how the rationalists were winning the fight for people's minds. On New Year's Eve 1899 he wrote a prayer to the Lord for the coming century: "Listen, how Science wildly raves. Around the altars overthrown. Brute Nature, with the world for slaves, Is God alone! Not made in God's own image now Is Man— 'tis thus the wise dispute'— But sprung from one same cell, they vow, Are Man and Brute."

Holy Mother Church was quick to see and respond to the errors that were spreading in academic circles. These errors, the popes understood, would have profound influence on the lives of men, especially on the their immortal souls, because a reduction of all human thought to only the physical reality is, by default, a denial of God. If one starts with a denial of God, how can they be saved? If there is no God, how can anyone sin against Him, let alone ask Him for forgiveness?

Pope St. Pius X recognized Modernism to be the "synthesis of all errors". In 1907, he wrote "evolution is the principle doctrine of the modernists... lay down the general principle that in a living religion everything is subject to change.... To the laws of evolution everything is subject under the penalty of death— dogma, Church, worship, the Books we revere as sacred, even faith itself." *Pascendi Dominici Gegis*, par. 26. In 1908, George Tyrell (1861-1909) and Alred Loisy (1857-1940) were both excommunicated for putting forward the idea of the "evolution of Christianity". Both died unwilling to recant their heretical claims. In 1910, the "Oath Against Modernism" was required for Catholic clergy and anyone teaching or writing. Unfortunately, naturalistic Darwinism was not clearly condemned as part of this heresy, and the poison continued to destroy minds and souls in the Church.

In the next chapter, we will see the real world applications of these ideas. They will be progressed by Marx and others, and will culminate in the World Wars. Remember that ideas have consequences, even false, erroneous ideas.

Chapter 6
How did we get here? Part Four
From Marx to the War to End All Wars

In this chapter we will see the real world application of the ideas of Kantian Materialism, mixed in with a healthy dose of Darwinian evolution. Karl Marx will start us off with his destructive ideas about the economy and politics. Next, we will see how these ideas spread through education and become enshrined in laws. These ideas will be applied to the elimination of certain groups of peoples, including the systematic killing of peoples in death camps and eugenics for those places for which these camps aren't feasible. Finally, we will see how countries send millions of men to fight each other in battle to the death, the war to end all wars, but not the final war? Ideas have consequences.

Let's take over and steal stuff from rich people, then kill them

In 1848, Karl Marx wrote his *Communist Manifesto*, but it needed work. After he read Darwin, he wrote his three-volume *Das Capital* 1867-83, that incorporated the ideas of Darwin with Calvinism and rationalistic Materialism, all into his own grand idea. Marx wrote to a friend in 1861, "Darwin's book is very important and serves me as a basis in natural selection for the class struggle in history.... Despite all deficiencies, not only is a death blow dealt here for the first time to 'Teleology' in the natural science, but their rational meaning is empirically explained."

Of course, Socialism was not a new idea. Someone taking from someone else for the greater good is as old as man. Even the fictitious Robin Hood was based on this idea. Marx twisted the idea of "survival of the fittest", which is observed in nature, and applied it to society. In his usage, however, the fittest are the "oppressed" or the poor, the workers. They are to attack and kill the "oppressors" or the rich, the people with money. This is a perversion of what we see in nature. In the realm of animals, the strong feed on the weak. He would have the lower, weaker economically, feed on the stronger, the rich. He ignores the symbiotic relationship of the boss or owner and the hired hand. This unnatural way of life simply replaces free enterprise bosses with government bosses, and the poor day laborer ends up worse for it, while still doing the same job, without even the option to quit. The communists tell people what job they have and how much they are compensated.

Marx added an atheistic government with the abolition of personal property. The spark for this change is the Marxist idea of class struggle, the oppressed versus the oppressors. At Marx's graveside Friedrich Engels noted, "Just as Darwin discovered the law of evolution in organic nature, so Marx discovered the law of evolution in human history." Now we see the rise of not just a secular government which ignores the Divine but a government which actively seeks to destroy the Church and the faith of Catholics.

A true fight to the death had begun. Marx knew that faith in God had to be destroyed. If the goodness of man comes from God, and man has dignity and rights because of this, then there is a natural line that no ruler can cross. As this is unacceptable for Marx, faith in God must be replaced by faith in the State. Thus enabled the State can, indeed must, control every aspect of life. Even whether you should live or die. The driving force for the communist is "what is best for the State", not "what is best for man". If there is no God that created man, and thus is the source of man's inalienable dignity, then the State must now be that source and thus has the "right" to give and take at its pleasure.

Of course this is nonsense, as a "State" is a construct of man for proper governance. We see here that a few "elite" set themselves up in the place of God, and rule like tyrants over the very people they proclaim to be helping better their lives. History has shown time and again that when government steps in to make life better, the opposite happens. The reason for this is that government bureaucrats and intellectual elites lack the practical knowledge to run actual businesses and services that are of true benefit. This is an example of the principle of subsidiarity not being used. Subsidiarity is the idea that things should run, be managed, at the lowest possible point that they can be. Parents should run their house, mayors should run their cities, governors should run their states, etc. The people on the ground have the practical knowledge to be successful in running their own lives, not a think-tank hundreds or thousands of miles away.

Great ideas, let's be sure to teach them to everyone, and change the laws

The materialist rationalists expanded their ideas into education and law next. In 1869, Charles Eliot became president of Harvard Law, and in 1870, Christopher Langdell became Dean of Harvard Law. Eliot wrote "...physics with its law of conservation of energy, chemistry with its doctrine of indestructibility and eternal flux of atoms, and biology with its principle of evolution through natural selection, have brought about within thirty years a wonderful change in men's conception of the universe. If the universe, as science teaches, be an organism which has by slow degrees grown to its form of today on its way to its form of tomorrow, with slowly formed habits which we call laws... then, as science also teaches, the life-principle of soul of that organism for which science has no better name than god, pervades and informs it so absolutely that there is no separating god from nature." Thus he saw the need to separate both the laws of nature, and laws of man, from God. Thus the reputable Harvard Law became a major source of changing the very outlook of law in the West.

Langdell was able to apply the idea of evolution to jurisprudence. Langdell wrote in 1879, "Law, considered as a science, consists of certain principles or doctrines.... Each of these doctrines has arrived at its present state by slow degrees; in other words, it is a growth, extending in many cases through centuries. This growth is to be traced in the main through a series of cases; and much the shortest the best, if not the only way of mastering the doctrine effectively, is by studying the case in which it is embodied." Here we see the idea of "case study" as the new way of evaluating and applying the law. Instead of going back to the law itself as it was intended by the law-giver, now they can look at cases as they are decided to apply the law. This leads to the situation we see today whereby judges are making laws that by any standard are contrary to the laws on the books. NB- It is often taught that this model of legal application was instituted at the founding of the US, but the reality is that it started in the late 19th century.

Langdell thought that as humans are a result of evolution so society is also evolving, and the laws must reflect the evolution of that society and evolve themselves. This happens by a simple change in emphasis from looking at how a law was written for its meaning and application, now to how it has been decided by the courts, called "case study". Thus over time, as cases came and interpreted previous cases, they moved further and further from the original law. This is a clever way to take the law-givers out of the loop, replacing them with judges.

As the heads of a preeminent school, these men were able to spread their errors, not only all over the US, but also all over the world. Graduates of this school, especially law, were able to gain places as elevated as the Supreme Court. The result is what we have seen. Instead of the theory of law based mainly on the Catholic principle in which man-made law is based on natural law with its inherent dependence on God, now law was being based solely on man. Thus these "lawyers" successfully changed the nature of law to now "evolve" and conform to whatever they would like. Judicial activism then emerged where judges now decide on their own what a law should mean and how to implement it.

This is how we have gotten to the point today where a child's rights can be subordinated to the rights of a mother to the point that a mother can willfully kill her own child if she chooses. Even the most basic reality of man that he is either man or woman, is now changed by a man simply choosing to be whatever they want. The very basis of society, a husband and wife with children, which is so necessary for the propagation of society, is now changed to allow for people of the same sex to claim this status. Even more bewildering is how some people have decided to "marry" irrational creatures such as dogs, cats, birds, dolphins, and more. As the law is no longer tied to natural law, anything goes. The old Greeks summed it up best when they defined "bad" as "anything that someone does not like", and "good" as "anything that makes someone 'happy'".

It's about time to overthrow a czar, and kill anyone that doesn't like it

Lenin ruled the Communist party in Russia from 1917-24 and liked to have a statuette of an ape holding a human skull, which was sitting on some books including Darwin's, on his desk. John Koster explained in *The Atheist Syndrome,* "The ape and the skull were a symbol of his faith, the Darwinian faith that man is brute, the world is a jungle, and individual lives are irrelevant."[vi] Stalin admitted that he lost his faith as a youth after he read Darwin. Years later in China, Mao Zedong noted that Darwinism was the foundation of Chinese scientific Socialism, and it was the first thing in which the Chinese communists indoctrinated people. The goal for them was the destruction of religious beliefs. Convincing people that they came from apes negates God, the soul, and eternal life. Having destroyed true Faith, Communism replaces it with a false one: Communist government. Bishop Cuthbert O'Gara, a prisoner in China, wrote in *The Surrender to Secularism*, "In the Red prison in which I was held, the slogan, 'Bring your mind over to us, and all your troubles will end', was hammered into the minds of the prisoners with brutal and numbing monotony."[vii] Some estimate the Chinese communists killed over 40 million in these prisons, but I think it's closer to 200 million or more. Even these horrific numbers pale in comparison to worse evils still active. I am not here denying or belittling the millions of people currently imprisoned and often killed by communists today.

Marxism more than any other error took the materialist attack against religion and spread it from the Church and Her philosophy to the normal lives of lay-people subject to the Church. To implement the Marxist idea required the removal of the normal freedoms and rights that people have. This includes the right to own private property, manage your own business, educate your own children, and the like. Of course, many people are not willing to give up these normal aspects of life. The communists had to forcibly abolish them, then round up and eliminate those many who complained about it. Some estimate on the low end that the communists in Russia killed around 80 to 100 million in order to implement this plan, others say that 250 million is a still low number. Conservative numbers these days estimate that worldwide Communism killed over 150 million by the turn of the last century.

The fact that many millions had to be eliminated to make this idea have power only illustrates how terribly bad the idea is. If you have to kill that many people for others to no longer fight against it, how good of an idea is it?

There are too many poor fools around here, let's kill them

Francis Galton, the father of eugenics, a cousin of Darwin,

worked to apply the ideas of natural selection to help move evolution forward with the help of man, in a similar way that horses, or dogs have been bred. In 1869's *Hereditary Genius,* Galton wrote, "if talented men were mated with talented woman, of some mental and physical characters as themselves, generation after generation, we might produce a highly bred human race, with no more tendency to revert to meaner ancestral types than is shown by our long-established breeds of race-horses and fox-hounds."[viii] Hebert Spencer made these ideas more widely accepted. In his reflections on sociology he wrote "Fostering the good-for-nothing at the expense of the good, is an extreme cruelty... There is no greater curse to posterity than that of bequeathing them an increasing population of imbeciles and idlers and criminals. To aid the bad in multiplying, is, in effect, the same as maliciously providing for our descendants a multitude of enemies." Spencer coined the phrase, "survival of the fittest".

In 1907, Galton helped form the Eugenics Education Society in England with the goal to propagandize the public. This group led to the 1923 founding of the American Eugenics Society that helped make almost 350 Universities offer courses in eugenics before WW2. Also, starting with Indiana in 1907, 28 states passed laws that forced sterilization in certain cases. By 1941 about 41,000 people were forcibly sterilized in the US. In 1927, the case *Buck vs. Bell* upheld in the Supreme Court the legality of states to do this. Justice Oliver Wendell Holmes wrote, "the public welfare may call upon the best citizens for their lives. It would be strange if it could not call upon those who already sap the strength of the State for these lesser sacrifices... in order to prevent our being swamped with incompetence.... The principle that sustains compulsory vaccination is broad enough to cover cutting the Fallopian tubes."

In the 1920 book, *Women and the New Race,* Margaret Sanger wrote, "The most merciful thing that the large family does to one of its infant members is to kill it."[ix] She started her first birth control shop in 1916 and in 1922, she started the American Birth Control league. It changed to Birth Control Federation of America in 1939, and then to Planned Parenthood Federation of America in 1942, its current name.

After the stories of eugenics in WW2 Europe, the Western movement stalled for a time. What they needed was to change the vocabulary so that it sounded like compassion. Who would want a child to grow up that is "unwanted or poor? Evolution is the theory that underpins the ideas of these people. They believed that evolution in humans has resulted in some humans being "more evolved" and thus more valuable. In this light is easy to see why they had no problem with killing the "lesser humans".

Thus we see with eugenics the ideas of Darwin and the like being applied. When people no longer see the goodness in their fellow men, that everyone is just a smarter ape, then it could make sense to actively try to kill the ones you find of little worth. Of course for those with Divine Faith who see all humans as a gift from God, with dignity, this is terrible.

I'm sick of the old ways, let's kill our society as well

In 1911 a German General F. Von Bernhardi wrote in *Germany and the Next War*, "War is a biological necessity of the first importance, a regulative element in the life of mankind which cannot be dispensed with, since without it an unhealthy development will follow.... The struggle for existence is, in the life of Nature, the basis of all healthy development.... Without war, inferior or decaying races would easily choke the growth of healthy budding elements, and a universal decadence would follow.... The natural law, to which all laws of Nature can be reduced, is the law of struggle.... This struggle is a creator, since it eliminates. Strong, healthy, and flourishing nations increase in numbers. From a given moment they require a continual expansion of their frontiers; they require new territory for the accommodation of their surplus population. Since every part of the planet is inhabited, new territory must, as a rule, be obtained... by conquest.... [War] is not only a biological law, but a moral obligation, and, as such, an indispensable factor in civilization."[x] This is an example of the rationalist and materialist logical conclusion that led to the hyper Nationalism that enabled the bloodshed of WWI. I seem to remember a warning about this from Our Lady.

Kaiser Wilhelm II thought that most Germans believed they needed more land so they were justified in simply taking it, and as he thought his people were superior, the war would be over in six weeks. The war, however, was a chastisement for not respecting Sunday, the Lord's Day, and for blasphemies. The war ended over four *years* later with about 17 million military and civilian deaths on the fronts. These results did nothing to slow the rationalist ideas down. These same ideas were given a round two in WW2. Hitler thought that this time the Germans would win by an application of natural selection. The German leadership continued to fight to the bitter end when the war turned badly. Many Germans noted at the time that they believed the "will to win" would enable them to triumph. This "will", of course, is the confusion of Nietszche lived out in the real world.

The fascist race ideas came from the rationalist/materialist ideology resulting in eugenics. The application of eugenics led to forced sterilization, abortion, etc. Hitler noted in the 1930's that he got his eugenics ideas from America, whom he admired and said was more advanced than Germany at the time. After almost six years of fighting, about 100 million people had died due to the war. WW2 was yet another chastisement for the lack of conversion from the offenses that people committed, with a similar result as WWI. I think we could say that, as men turned away from God, they turned to themselves, to the State. This apostasy away from the Church is most dire.

At this time rationalist ideas had reached many quarters of the Western world. There was a sense that man had or nearly had the power to remake the world and fix all problems on his own. By the turn of the previous century, Nationalism as we know it, with an emphasis of putting your hopes and trust in the nation-state, was almost complete. This was contradictory to the classic Christian disposition of putting your hope and trust in God.

In this light, we can better understand the arrogant thoughts of the people that actually thought they could fight in a "war to end all wars". It seems the lesson the Lord was trying to give the world at that time was how disastrous life would turn out if man put their hopes in government "of man, by man, and for man". Here, too, the lesson was lost.

Christ the King is the source of all authority. He is the only answer to all the travails of this life.

In the next chapter we will look at Our Lady of Fatima and the greatest public miracle since the parting of the Red Sea by Moses.

Chapter 7
Our Lady of Fatima[xi], 1917, 1929

In this chapter we will look at the apparitions of Our Lady of Fatima, Portugal. This apparition was the in-between of the 19th and 20th centuries. By the end of the 19th century, ideas absolutely opposed to Church teaching were having their consequences all across Europe and in people's lives individually. Heaven came in the form of Our Lady, as a warning, at the beginning of the largest consequence of these ideas, the World Wars.

A Plea from the Pope, Heaven responds

Pope Benedict XV called WWI the "suicide of western civilization". On May 5th, 1917, he pleaded with Our Blessed Lord and Our Lady to intervene and stop the bloodshed. Eight days after his plea, Our Lady appeared in Fatima, Portugal. She called for conversion, penance, and the consecration of Russia. She warned that if her request was not heeded, a worse chastisement in the form of another large war would ensue. Her warnings were not heeded. WWII occurred. However, even after this far more deadly war and the advent of atheistic governments that went a step beyond the Nationalism of the West, by outlawing Christianity and presenting themselves as the end-all-be-all for everyone, the lesson of misplaced trust and confidence in man-made institutions was still not learned. Nor were the more vital lesson of the repercussions of offending God.

Our Lady gave the solution to these problems and promised that if the pope and bishops did what She requested, the consecration of Russia to Her Immaculate Heart, a miraculous conversion would occur, and there would be peace. Again, She warned that if this did not happen another worse chastisement, now the third in recent years, would be worse than the deluge. This in part is due to the fact that the world is now worse than it was at the time of the Great Deluge (the Flood). She promised that in the end the pope with all the bishops would indeed consecrate Russia, then there would be peace, and Her Immaculate Heart would triumph.

Our Lady of Fatima, May 13 - Oct. 13, 1917

Our Lady appeared to the children from May to October 1917,

once a month on the 13th of each month, except for one, August, because the masonic mayor had them confined in jail. However, Our Lady on Aug. 19 consoled the children, abjured them to pray and do penance, and promised that in October She would perform a miracle to prove that the apparitions are real. Also, She promised that St. Joseph would bring the Baby Jesus, and Our Lady of the Rosary, of Sorrows, and of Carmel would also come. Here we will focus on the "Secret", given on July 13, 1917, and the "Miracle of the Sun" that occurred on October 13, 1917. There are many sources that cover the whole episode and even the rest of the lives of these three children. Cf- *The True Story of Fatima*, by John de Marchi, I.M.C.

The Secret imparted to the three shepherd children at Fatima on July 13, 1917 had three parts. The first part was fully revealed in Sr. Lucy's Third and Fourth *Memoirs*, written at the command of her bishop, in 1941. This is one apparition that is divided into three parts for ease of study. About 5,000 people were present.

First Secret

This first part of the Secret of Fatima describes what Lucy, Jacinta, and Francisco saw on that day. From Sister Lucy's memoirs:

"She [Our Lady of Fatima] opened Her hands once more, as She had done during the two previous months. The rays of light seemed to penetrate the earth, and we saw as it were a sea of fire. Plunged in this fire were demons and souls [of the damned] in human form, like transparent burning embers, all blackened or burnished bronze, floating about in the conflagration, now raised into the air by the flames that issued from within themselves together with great clouds of smoke, now falling back on every side like sparks in huge fires, without weight or equilibrium, amid shrieks and groans of pain and despair, which horrified us and made us tremble with fear. (It must have been this sight which caused me to cry out, as people say they heard me). The demons could be distinguished [from the souls of the damned] by their terrifying and repellent likeness to frightful and unknown animals, black and transparent like burning coals."[xii] "This vision lasted but an instant. How can we ever be grateful enough to our kind heavenly Mother, Who had already prepared us by promising, in the first apparition, to take us to Heaven. Otherwise, I think we would have died of fear and terror."[xiii]

Our Lady then explained to the children, "You have seen hell where the souls of poor sinners go."

Comments

Our Lady showed the children a vision of Hell, the children being seven (Jacinta), eight (Francisco), and ten years (Lucia) old. I note this here because Our Lady had no problem revealing the reality of Hell to these children, and they had no problem with this truth. Of course, they were shocked and frightened, but look at their response: a deeper faith, more intense prayer, and penance. This first vision is a possible end. That is to say that Hell is a real place and that actual people go if they do not heed the words of Our Lord and Our Lady. Also it should not be lost on us that a bit of Hell was at that time unleashed on earth, in the form of WWI.

Second Secret

Our Lady then confided to them the second part of the Secret. This second part primarily concerns Heaven's requests for the Consecration of Russia to the Immaculate Heart of Mary and for the Communions of Reparation on the First Saturdays and the consequences of failing to heed these requests. As recorded in Sister Lucy's memoirs, the second part of the Secret is as follows:

"To save them [poor sinners who are on the road to hell], God wishes to establish in the world devotion to My Immaculate Heart. If what I say to you is done, many souls will be saved, and there will be peace. The war is going to end; but if people do not cease offending God, a worse war will break out during the reign of Pius XI. When you see a night illumined by an unknown light, know that this is the great sign given you by God that He is about to punish the world for its crimes, by means of war, famine, and persecutions against the Church and against the Holy Father.

"To prevent this, I shall come to ask for the consecration of Russia to My Immaculate Heart, and the Communion of Reparation on the First Saturdays. If My requests are heeded, Russia will be converted, and there will be peace; if not, she will spread her errors throughout the world, causing wars and persecutions against the Church. The good will be martyred, the Holy Father will have much to suffer, various nations will be annihilated.[xiv]

"In the end, My Immaculate Heart will triumph. The Holy Father will consecrate Russia to Me, and she will be converted, and a period of peace will be granted to the world."

Comments

One might ask why devotion to the Immaculate Heart now? Did not the Church declare the Immaculate Conception already? Of course, however, Our Lord clearly wants to have Our Lady receive the honors, respect, love, and devotion which She deserves. In an interview which Sr. Lucy gave decades later, she says that Our Lady revealed that Satan was in a mood for a final fight with Our Lady, and the Lord is allowing this fight to take place. In this context we must remember that the fallen angels have been fighting the Kingdom of God from the moment they were kicked out of Heaven by St. Michael and his angels. One might say that Our Lord, by allowing the fallen to have a greater sway over humans, is both teaching the world our great need for the Queen of Heaven, and the results of what happens when we do not have recourse to Her aid and guidance. Of course any saint from the time of the resurrection is very well aware of the need for Our Lady, Her perfection, and Her love. Now that thousands of saints have come and gone, teaching and preaching on the necessity to have a true devotion to Our Lady, how many Catholics pray their rosary every day? How many Catholics have a true daily devotion to the Immaculate Heart, let alone the Sacred Heart? Heaven wants to change all that.

Our Lady reveals the end of WWI, a call for repentance, and, at the same time, a warning that if people do not repent and change their sinful ways, a worse war will break out. She even gives a timeframe, "during the reign of Pius XI"; we call it WWII. It was preceded by a night illumined by an unknown light, which was reported by the newspapers all over Europe and the US. Some say that the timing is wrong because Germany attacked Poland in September 1939, and the Pope died in February. True, however, the decision by Hitler was clearly made before February and in any event the Japanese had started fighting the Chinese and then the Russians years before. On Nov. 5th 1937, Hitler laid out his plans for future wars to the leaders of Germany. The memo is called *The Hossbach Memorandum*. Remember that sin is marked from the moment the decision is made, not when the act is carried out, or even if one is successful in carrying out the act. So yes, Our Lady was right, "during the reign of Pius XI".

Our Lady did not leave us without a remedy. The answer is for the pope with all the bishops to consecrate Russia to Her Immaculate Heart and for the laity to make First Saturday Communions of Reparation. She says that She will come back later to ask for this. This makes sense. The Communist Revolution had not even started in Russia by July of 1917; it would not start until that October. Our Lady gives a dire warning that if She is not heeded, Russia "will spread her errors throughout the world, causing wars and persecution against the Church. The good will be martyred, the Holy Father will have much to suffer, various nations will be annihilated." Here She is talking about the time after WWII.

Let us now take this warning, as it is laid out, in turn. The "errors of Russia": First; Russia had become a schismatic state, separated from the proper leadership of the pope, not in daily governance, but in matters of the Faith. Second; there was a Nationalism rising up that replaced the rule of Christ the King with the state; the Orthodox have a history of subordinating their church to the State. Under the communists, they would take it a step further to the separation of Church and State. Third; with the rise of Communism, many other things would come about that are antithetical to true religion. For example, by 1920, abortion on demand was legal, as was homosexuality and pornography, there was a loss of the right to own private property, and atheism was the only accepted belief for the comrades. Also, they promoted promiscuity even for those that were married.

Within a few years the Marxists had to reverse these trends (promiscuity, homosexuality, pornography, and unlimited abortions) because they found that these major disruptions to the home led to major disruptions in the workplace, military, etc. They learned a valuable lesson, and while they did not tolerate these ideas in their own land, they promoted them in other lands. Thus, all of the life-changing elements that are demanded by Communism also are part of the "errors" of Russia. Many mistakenly think that Communism and its implementation is the error. It is one error, but the attacks on the Faith and the family are far more devastating.

Only a cursory glance at history after WWII reveals the fulfillment of Our Lady's warning of "causing wars and persecutions against the Church", that "the good will be martyred, the Holy Father will have much to suffer". For example it is said that the Germans killed twelve million people in death camps, six million Jews and six million others. Many say that the majority of the "others" were Catholics. St. Maximilian Kolbe is included in this list. But this is only in Germany. How many Catholics were killed in Russia and China during those years? How many are still imprisoned by the communists today?

The other elements of Our Lady's warnings are sometimes considered to have been fulfilled as well. "The Holy Father will have much to suffer." The attempted assassination of Pope John Paul II comes to mind, on May 13th, 1981 (the anniversary of the first apparition at Fatima). He stated that it was the hand of Our Lady of Fatima that directed the bullet away from his heart and allowed him to survive. On May 12th, 1982, during a pilgrimage to Fatima where the Pope took the bullet and placed it on the Crown of the Statue of Our Lady of Fatima, he was stabbed. The wound was small, and the Pope had it bandaged so that he could still say the Mass that day.

Beyond these attempts, certainly we can say the popes have suffered. However, it seems the vision that is part of the third secret reveals that there are still greater sufferings of a pope that clearly has not yet happened. For instance, "the Holy Father passed through a big city half in ruins and half trembling with halting step, afflicted with pain and sorrow, he prayed for the souls of the corpses he met on his way; having reached the top of the mountain, on his knees at the foot of the big Cross he was killed by a group of soldiers who fired bullets and arrows at him." More on this secret below, but clearly a pope has not yet been killed by bullets and arrows.

"Various nations will be annihilated." Similar to the sufferings of the Holy Father, this very ominous warning may have been only partially fulfilled. For example, the communist state of Vietnam previously had been mostly communist, and while a government change such as this also changes the very nature of the society it governs, it could not be called annihilation. In this warning, nations are annihilated in that the very people are annihilated, not just suffering under a difficult change in governance. Historically, the Carthaginians were annihilated by the Romans. After the Punic

Wars, the nation of Carthage no longer existed. Even the Kingdom of France was annihilated by the masonic Bloody Revolution and turned into *Le Republic*. These are examples of annihilation which show it is not unheard of in history, and they happened before the apparition at Fatima. This part of the warning does not seem to have taken place, yet.

It also might be the case that none of the warnings about the martyrs, the Holy Father, or nations has happened even partially. Meaning that this warning is not about a series of events over decades but rather about a much shorter timeframe that has not begun. The events mentioned above, killing of Catholics thus far, the sufferings of the Pope, and some governmental changes to societies, are only a forewarning of far worse things yet to come.

It is a principle of prophesy that they are nearly impossible to interpret, in detail, until they are fulfilled. We can understand the overall message, meaning that the call to conversion, prayer, and penance is needed, but the central part of the message is the consecration of Russia. Only then will conversion and peace follow. Also, these prophesies are contingent. That is, if you don't do this, then this will happen, if you do this, then these punishments will be avoided, if you only do part of this, then the punishments will be mitigated (lessened). This will be more clearly seen below. This warning, in all likelihood, is predicting WWIII, which has obviously not happened, yet.

I want to make it clear that the center of the message is the consecration of Russia. If we take the warnings before this central message then it seems clear these warnings are about WWII and WWIII. On June 13, 1929, Our Lady came, as She promised, and said now is the time to consecrate Russia. By this time the USSR existed, and everyone in the world knew it was atheistic, materialist, and anti-Catholic. Thus, if the consecration had occurred, then the first part of that warning, WWII, would have been avoided. It did not happen, thus WWII.

The second part of the warning deals with the period after WWII. The "super powers" have been in one type of war with each other or their surrogate states nearly non-stop. They are often called "proxy" wars. Clearly, peace has not been granted, yet. By this I mean that, while the "Cold War" was declared over, it only shifted gears and became ever more covert. The Russians clearly stayed focused on the cultural war, and notice the results today. The US clearly stayed focused on international business. The only real change was a little less spending on guns and ships by both sides. Now, in recent decades the Chinese have become an actual military, financial, intelligence, and cultural influence. It can also be noted that there was no clear winner in WWII. In the end the main antagonist, USSR and USA were not only still standing but were more powerful than ever.

"In the end, My Immaculate Heart will triumph. The Holy Father will consecrate Russia to Me, and she will be converted, and a period of peace will be granted to the world." Clearly, here, we can see Our Lady is fortifying our faith and bolstering our hope so that no matter how long it takes for the pope and the bishops to do as they were requested, Her Immaculate Heart will triumph and peace will be granted. It is hard to imagine a world without wars.

You may ask, why is the consecration so vitally important to God? I can only give an informed opinion, but here it is. At the heart of the high priestly prayer of Our Lord in the Garden of Gethsemane on the night He was betrayed, according to the Gospel of St. John, is His prayer for unity. We know that when Our Lord prayed, asked, or spoke anything, it was and is immediately realized. Thus, the mystical Body, which is the Church, has always and will always be perfectly united. However, the Schismatics, while they are baptized, are not united to the Sea of St. Peter, the visible and actual Vicar of Christ. They are separated. This is called a schism. They are not a separate church, as though the Lord established separate bodies. No, they are outside the One, Holy, Catholic, and Apostolic Church. Thus, the pope and the bishops of the One Church doing this simple prayer will result in the conversion of this largest body of Christians outside the Church, by the intercession of Our Lady, and will once again show the world there is One God, One King, One Church, One Queen, and one way to heaven. This act will show the power and authority of the Magisterium with the pope and bishops united in one body. It will, in one fell swoop, reveal yet again, the Oneness of God to His Body, the Church, and result in the Honor that is due to Him and His Mother, our Queen, while at the same time showing the absolute necessity of Him and Her for salvation. Thus, we see frequent reference to devotion to His Sacred Heart and Her Immaculate Heart.

Third Secret

In her Fourth Memoir (dated December 8, 1941), Sister Lucy copied the first two parts of the Fatima Secret word-for-word, including what appears to be the conclusion to the whole Secret:

"In the end, My Immaculate Heart will triumph. The Holy Father will consecrate Russia to Me, and she will be converted, and a period of peace will be granted to the world."

Partial Text of the Third Secret

Sister Lucy then immediately added the following text to her Fourth Memoir:

"In Portugal the dogma of the Faith will always be preserved etc."

Fatima scholars have been unanimous in their belief that this phrase begins the third part of the Secret and the word "etc." that Sister Lucy wrote indicates the rest of the words Our Lady spoke in the text of the Third Secret. Here it must be noted that immediately following the words, "In Portugal the dogma of the Faith will always be preserved etc.", Our Lady said to Sister Lucy: "Tell this to no one. Yes you may tell it to Francisco." The "this" that can be told to Francisco refers to the last thing said during the vision. If it was only a vision, without an explanation, then Francisco didn't need to be told anything, because he had just seen it himself already. But if "this" refers to additional words of the Virgin by way of explanation of the vision, then Francisco would have to be told because, as we know, he could not hear Our Lady during the Fatima apparitions. Francisco *saw* but did not *hear*, and would thus have needed to be informed about what Our Lady had *said* about the vision.

Nor can one argue plausibly that "you may tell it to Francisco" refers merely to the words Our Lady spoke during the second part of the Secret. The phrase, "Tell this to no one. Yes, you may tell it to Francisco", follows immediately after "In Portugal the dogma of the Faith will always be preserved etc." Clearly, then, the "etc." indicates the words, not yet written down, that Sister Lucy could *tell* Francisco orally. Those words clearly belong to the Third Secret, which was finally written down in 1944 under orders from the Bishop of Fatima. In any event this line is most ominous. If Portugal is able to retain the faith, good for them, then *de facto*

84

other nations will not preserve the faith. I have noted above the false part of the apparition of La Salette that wrongly claims that Rome will lose the faith. But given the brevity of the third secret, it seems the list of places not to lose the faith is very short. Without the rest of the explanation of the secret, what more can be said with certainty?

<u>Vatican's Version of the Third Secret, Released June 26, 2000</u>
On June 26, 2000, the Vatican released what they claim to be the "third part" of the Secret of Fatima, given by Our Lady to the three shepherd children on July 13, 1917, but this text contains no actual words of Our Lady indicated by the "etc.". The text that the Vatican released is as follows:

"After the two parts which I have already explained, at the left of Our Lady and a little above, we saw an Angel with a flaming sword in his left hand; flashing, it gave out flames that looked as though they would set the world on fire; but they died out in contact with the splendor that Our Lady radiated towards him from her right hand: pointing to the earth with his right hand, the Angel cried out in a loud voice: Penance, Penance, Penance!. And we saw in an immense light that is God: something similar to how people appear in a mirror when they pass in front of it, a Bishop dressed in White, we had the impression that it was the Holy Father. Other Bishops, Priests, men and women Religious going up a steep mountain, at the top of which there was a big Cross of rough-hewn trunks as of a cork-tree with the bark; before reaching there the Holy Father passed through a big city half in ruins and half trembling with halting step, afflicted with pain and sorrow, he prayed for the souls of the corpses he met on his way; having reached the top of the mountain, on his knees at the foot of the big Cross he was killed by a group of soldiers who fired bullets and arrows at him, and in the same way there died one after another the other Bishops, Priests, men and women Religious, and various lay people of different ranks and positions. Beneath the two arms of the Cross there were two Angels, each with a crystal aspersorium in his hand, in which they gathered up the blood of the Martyrs and with it sprinkled the souls that were making their way to God."

<u>Commentary</u>
As stated above it seems nonsense to argue that the entire third

secret has been given to the public. In every other legitimate apparition when there is a vision, an explanation follows. Even in the first vision of Hell, that the children immediately understood to be Hell, Our Lady tells them that it is a vision of Hell. Also, Our Lady tells Lucy to go ahead and tell Francisco what She said, as he had already seen what the Vatican released above.

This vision is an incredibly long, detailed, and nuanced view into the future. Some aspects seem clear, others seem hard to understand, and as a whole what can we really make of it? We need the explanation of Our Lady. As a loving Mother who pointed out the obviousness of Hell, it is unthinkable that She would not explain this dire vision.

In any event, I will make a few comments on the vision. As to the scene; Our Lady is flanked by an angel with a flaming sword to her left, and, with what seems to be mercy coming from Her right hand, She is able to quell the flame. The flame must be God's justice. The angel points down to Earth with his free right hand and "cries out", if crying out is not descriptive enough, with a "loud voice: Penance, Penance, Penance!". Immediately I am reminded of the threefold betrayal of St. Peter during the Passion, and the Lord's threefold question and healing or feeding of the lambs and sheep on the shore of the sea of Tiberius, (John 21ff) when St. Peter reaffirms his love for God and is given the mandate to govern the Church. Could this indicate a betrayal from the pope or from some in the upper Hierarchy?

Then there is "an immense light that is God". Here I think she is trying to explain an aspect of the beatific vision, a view of reality from the Divine perspective. This is also to indicate that what follows is of a more sublime and elevated nature than what was seen before. Think of it this way, when they see Our Lady and the angel they are looking "beyond the veil" that separates our physical sight from our spiritual sight. This is a glimpse of the preternatural. Now, with the immense light, the children are looking beyond the preternatural into the supernatural, not as much with the eyes of the body, as before, but now with the eyes of the soul.

"Something similar to how people appear in a mirror when they pass in front of it, a Bishop dressed in White; we had the impression that it was the Holy Father." This sentence I think is saying the same thing twice. In the first half it is clear that there is a Bishop in White— interesting that there is the capital letter indicating a title— if the Pope, why not say so? This is a "reflection" of the real thing but not the actual thing, just as anything reflected is not the actual thing but looks like it. Also, this could show that at the same time there is an actual Pope, there will be another Bishop that dresses and acts like the Pope, although he is not the Pope. Then they, "had the impression that it was the Holy Father". The word "impression" seems to indicate that there is a clear attempt at looking like, or having the outward appearance of someone, but the children might have known that he was a fake. Note that Holy Father is only mentioned at the end, indicating that before this the children are trying to figure out who this man is and who he is trying to imitate. Only at the end do they realize he is trying to be the Pope, like a bad skit that someone has to explain.

"Other Bishops, Priests, men and women Religious going up a steep mountain, at the top of which there was a big Cross of rough-hewn trunks as of a cork-tree with the bark." This man already mentioned is clearly a Bishop, along with other Bishops, Priests, Religious on a kind of pilgrimage up a mountain to a "big Cross" that is roughly made. This cross is without a corpus. As if to say that they follow this cross devoid of the suffering Christ. Also, this cross is described, in some detail, as seemingly hastily made and not very attractive, poor craftsmanship. What or who is Christ without the cross? What is the cross without Christ? Another religion, certainly not Catholic.

I think this first part is about a group of Bishops with others that are trying to usurp and change the true Faith to make it devoid of Christ. The mountain is steep and the only thing on it is a rough cross. It seems the mountain is outside the city and totally devoid of life. The mountain and cross are mentioned before the destruction and death. Thus indicating that this group had a plan before the destruction, and so I conclude, they are the cause of the destruction and deaths. Literally the "march" of this cadre is followed immediately by a description of destruction. One follows the other. Meaning that the group, while moving through the City of God, are in fact destroying it and killing holy people along "their way".

"Before reaching there the Holy Father passed through a big city half in ruins and half trembling with halting step, afflicted with pain and sorrow, he prayed for the souls of the corpses he met on his way." It is clear to the children that it is in fact the Holy Father.

That is to say there is no doubt that the Holy Father will travel through some place that is devastated, he will be nearly overcome, he is barely able to walk, he is afflicted with personal pain and spiritual turmoil, and he advances to meet and pray for the bodies he encounters. Is this city actually a metaphor for a country, a continent, western civilization, the world, perhaps Christendom, or maybe even the City of God? I have to say it is too unclear without the explanation. That half of this "city" is destroyed is fearsome.

This "city half in ruins" makes me recall the parable of the man left half-dead in St. Luke's Gospel, Chapter Ten. In this parable, a man goes down from Jerusalem, is robbed, and left half-dead on the side of the road. An aspect of this parable is that the man is symbolic of fallen humanity, half-dead, meaning that physically he is alive but spiritually dead. Hence the need of fallen man for new life offered in Christ through Baptism, nourished and kept alive in the Church.

Could this mean that "The Church" symbolized by the "The City of God "now looks like She always did from the outside, but in fact is spiritually dead? Has She been robbed of Her true goodness and gifts? That the pope will suffer is the next truth that comes through. It seems he will suffer in every way: physically, mentally, spiritually, and emotionally. Remember Our Lady prophesied that the pope would have to suffer much. He then prays for the souls of the corpses he met on his way. Is this phrase "his way" to make a distinction from "The Way" that is Christ? These dead could be the faithful Catholics that fought the insurrection that worked to change and destroy the faith. If we link "his way" with the ugly-looking cross bereft of Christ and the city being "The City of God", then these dead could be victims of an "anti-Church" that is the source of the destruction and the death.

"Having reached the top of the mountain, on his knees at the foot of the big Cross he was killed by a group of soldiers who fired bullets and arrows at him, and in the same way there died one after another the other Bishops, Priests, men and women Religious, and various lay people of different ranks and positions." This seems to indicate that the pope with the others, will, in fact, reach the goal for which they had set out. Also this mountain seems to be outside the city. However, having reached the goal, they are summarily struck down.

Is this to show that when it looks like the enemies of the Church have won, in fact they will have lost? This, of course, is the continuation of my own interpretation that the above-mentioned cross is symbolic of an attempt to alter the Faith, the cross without Christ. But clearly this shows an organized group that kills many bishops, priests, religious, and laity, but outside the City of God. Is the action of the pope to kneel and pray a sign of a change of mind, a kind of reconciliation and possible conversion of the Holy Father with the timeless Faith of the Ages?

In this moment of apparent victory, having reached the summit, this group is summarily annihilated. Is this a warning against people of all ranks seeking the cross without Christ, thinking there is salvation without the Passion, when there is, in fact, no peace outside the City of God?

"Beneath the two arms of the Cross there were two Angels, each with a crystal aspersorium in his hand, in which they gathered up the blood of the Martyrs and with it sprinkled the souls that were making their way to God." The vision ends on a note of hope. We see here that there are people making their way to God, Heaven exists, and people do go there. However it seems to indicate that this group which is killed is being sprinkled by the blood of the martyrs which were first encountered by the pope on his way to the cross. Thus those holy ones that died fighting this group are actually the source of grace for the conversion of this group that is killed at the foot of the cross.

I say this because in the Sacred Text and Tradition when the blood of the martyrs is mentioned, their blood is always recovered in a chalice, or at least that is what I recall. An aspersorium is the bucket or vessel that is used to sprinkle liquid, usually holy water, in the liturgy. Thus, the blood which is sprinkled by the angels here has already been collected. The blood of the martyrs could have been "collected" or transferred from the chalice to the aspersorium. It is definitely not their blood, meaning not the blood of the group reaching the summit.

In a more disastrous interpretation, this part could mean that while these poor souls are dying they realize their mistakes by seeing that the blood of the martyrs is being dispensed to other souls and not to them. I have already noted that the blood of those on the summit is not being gathered, and the blood of the holy martyrs is not clearly given to them. Also the martyrs are never sprinkled with the blood of other martyrs. Why would they be? They are martyrs themselves already.

I have to admit that this interpretation could be totally wrong, especially in the details. I do think that some aspects might be on the right track. We will have to see. However, let's imagine for a moment that my way of thinking is not too far off. What is Our Lady trying to show us with this vision? Remember this was in 1917, and WWI would rage for another year and half, while WWII with all the carnage and bombs had not yet happened. The idea that the pope, and many bishops and priests, etc., would work together and be the cause of great destruction in the world, let alone the Church, was unimaginable. Today, it's not so hard to imagine.

It is often said that as the Church goes, so goes the world. All we have to do is look around and see where we are to know how we got here. Something horrifically terrible has happened to the Church, and the world has followed suit.

The Miracle of the Sun, October 13, 1917

There were about 70,000 people present. Beginning the night before and persisting throughout the morning, a cold rain fell on the crowd. The ground was muddy, and the rain soaked everything. At the time when Our Lady was due to arrive, Lucy begged the people to close their umbrellas, which they did at once.

The miracle announced by Our Lady then took place: the sky abruptly cleared and the sun "danced". The people were able to look at the bright sun directly, without it bothering their eyes at all. A physician, Dr. Almeida Garrett, testified:

"Suddenly I heard the uproar of thousands of voices, and I saw the whole multitude spread out in that vast space at my feet... turn their backs to that spot where, until then, all their expectations focused, and look at the sun on the other side... I turned around, too, toward the point commanding their gazes, and I could see the sun, like a very clear disc, with its sharp edge, which gleamed without hurting the sight... It could not be confused with the sun seen through a fog (there was no fog at that moment), for it was neither veiled, nor dim. At Fatima, it kept its light and heat, and stood out clearly in the sky, with a sharp edge, like a large gaming table. The most astonishing thing was to be able to stare at the solar disc for a long time, brilliant with light and heat, without hurting the eyes, or damaging the retina."[xv]

The testimony of Avelino de Almeida, editor-in-chief of *O Seculo*, Lisbon's anticlerical and Masonic daily newspaper, is similar:

"And then we witnessed a unique spectacle, an incredible spectacle, unbelievable if you did not witness it. From above the road.... We see the immense crowd turn towards the sun, which appeared at its zenith, clear of the clouds. It looked like a plate of dull silver, and it was possible to stare at it without the least discomfort. It did not burn the eyes. It did not blind. One might say that an eclipse had occurred."[xvi]

Yet another astonishing aspect of the Miracle was that all of the thousands of people, most of whom were soaked to the bone and dirty from the mud, suddenly found that their clothes were dry and clean.

The academician Marques da Cruz testified:
"This enormous multitude was drenched, for it had rained unceasingly since dawn. But – though this may appear incredible — after the great miracle everyone felt comfortable, and found his garments quite dry, a subject of general wonder... The truth of this fact has been guaranteed with the greatest sincerity by dozens and dozens of persons of absolute trustworthiness, whom I have known intimately from childhood, and who are still alive [1937], as well as by persons from various districts of the country who were present."[xvii]

In one aspect, this is the most astonishing effect of the miracle and an indisputable proof of its authenticity: The amount of energy needed to accomplish this process of drying in a natural way and in such a short a time, would have incinerated everyone present at the time. As this aspect of the miracle contradicts the laws of nature radically, no demon could ever have achieved it.

Finally, many miracles of conversion, the greatest miracle God can bestow, also occurred. Here are two examples:

"The captain of the regiment of soldiers on the mountain that day— with orders to prevent the gathering of the crowd— was converted instantly. Apparently so were hundreds of other unbelievers, as their testimony will show."[xviii]

During the Miracle of the Sun, the three children were witnessing something else: the beautiful spectacle promised by Our Lady. Lucy writes:

"Our Lady having disappeared in the immensity of the firmament, we saw, beside the sun, Saint Joseph with the Child Jesus and Our Lady clothed in white with a blue mantle. Saint Joseph and the Child Jesus seemed to bless the world with gestures which they made with their hands in the form of a cross.

Soon after, that apparition having ceased, I saw Our Lord and Our Lady, Who gave me the impression of being Our Lady of Sorrows. Our Lord seemed to bless the world in the same manner as Saint Joseph.

That apparition disappeared, and it seemed to me that I saw Our Lady again, this time as Our Lady of Mount Carmel."

Commentary

These three successive visions are connected to one of the dominant messages of Fatima: the Rosary. In each of Her six apparitions, Our Lady asked that the Rosary be prayed, and here, in these visions granted to the three children, the mysteries of the Holy Rosary were represented. With the vision of the Holy Family we find the Joyful mysteries; the Sorrowful mysteries are represented by the vision of Our Lord and Our Lady of Sorrows; and the Glorious mysteries are represented in the vision of Our Lady of Mt. Carmel.

When the visions had disappeared, and the sun was again normal, Lucy was placed on the shoulder of a man in the crowd and carried safely through the masses to the road. As she was moving past the people, she cried out to them, pleading one of the important themes in the Fatima Message: to convert, return to God, and to flee sin. Her exact words were: "Do penance! Do penance! Our Lady wants you to do penance!", but Frère Michel states that in Portuguese this does not mean "performing mortifications", but rather "being converted, returning to God, fleeing sin". Through this plea, Lucy was reiterating the sorrowful request Our Lady had made of humanity in Her final apparition: "Do not offend the Lord our God anymore, because He is already too much offended."

Thus the Miracle of the Sun, witnessed by 70,000 people, concluded the cycle of the apparitions at Fatima. Yet the Message of Fatima, with its great depth and scope, was to continue to be unfolded to the eldest of the three seers, Lucy. In the years to come Heaven's Messenger would be visited and, as promised by Our Lady in the July 13th apparition, would be instructed to reveal Heaven's plan for peace for a turbulent world: the reparatory devotion of the Five First Saturdays and the consecration of Russia to the Immaculate Heart of Mary.

I believe that The Miracle of the Sun is the greatest public miracle performed since the Parting of the Red Sea during the Exodus. Public because the Incarnation and Resurrection were only shown to those chosen by God beforehand. In any event, this miracle is astounding in every way. Is this miracle, where so many thought they were going to die, in some way connected to the still hidden explanation of the Third Secret? I think Our Lady of Akita, Japan, will help answer this.

Our Lady of Fatima Timeline after 1917

1925, December 10: Our Lady appears to Sister Lucy at Pontevedra in Spain to relate the specific requirements for the Communion of Reparation on the First Saturdays. In the words of Our Lady:

"See, my daughter, my Heart encircled by thorns with which ungrateful men pierce it at every moment by their blasphemies and ingratitude. Do you, at least, strive to console me. Tell them that I promise to assist at the hour of death with the graces necessary for salvation all those who, in order to make reparation to me, on the First Saturday of five successive months, go to Confession, receive Holy Communion, say five decades of the Rosary, and keep me company for a quarter of an hour, meditating on the… mysteries of the Rosary."

1929, June 13: In fulfillment of Her promise at Fatima on July 13, 1917, Our Lady of Fatima appears to Sister Lucy at Tuy, Spain in the visible presence of the Most Holy Trinity and asks for the consecration of Russia to Her Immaculate Heart. In the words of Our Lady:

"This is the moment when God asks the Holy Father to make, in union with all the bishops of the world, the consecration of Russia to my Immaculate Heart.

"He promises to save it by that means. So many are the souls which the justice of God condemns for sins committed against me that I come to ask for reparation. Sacrifice yourself for this intention and pray."

Thus Our Lady gives three conditions for the Consecration: 1; the pope, 2; with all the bishops, and 3; consecrates Russia to Her Immaculate Heart.

Just a word on consecration and blessings in the Catholic Church: consecrate means to set aside and make holy, that is, to set aside for God for His use. It is a most solemn blessing. Babies are consecrated at baptism, churches and altars are consecrated for the holy sacraments, etc., the hands of priests are consecrated. Thus by asking for a consecration, Our Lady is saying that Russia is being given a huge blessing. Russia has been chosen for an important role in the Divine Plan of salvation. It's a gift from God, through the hands of Our Lady. Who in their right mind would not want to receive this gift, who would not want to be an agent to give it? Finally in this kind of act, consecration, the name of the person or place, in this case a nation, must be mentioned. If one is walking by a house and wants to give a gift to a person in it, they can't just throw the gift in the yard with no name. Also when one is baptized, the name must be said, or the baptism does not take place, it is the same with ordination and confirmation. Naming Russia with the bishops seems so simple, but it has not happened yet. Blessings are freely given by priests and bishops all the time to individuals and groups. These do not require names just the calling down of Divine grace. To consecrate a nation takes only a little more, the desire to consecrate and the name of the person or place.

1930

Why five First Saturdays in particular? Our Lord explained this to Sr. Lucy on May 29-30, 1930, saying:

"Daughter, the motive is simple: There are five kinds of offenses and blasphemies spoken against the Immaculate Heart of Mary.

"First: blasphemies against the Immaculate Conception;

"Second: against her Virginity;

"Third: against the Divine Maternity, refusing, at the same time, to receive her as the Mother of mankind;

"Fourth: those who seek publicly to implant, in the hearts of children, indifference, disrespect, and even hate for this Immaculate Mother;

"Fifth: those who revile her directly in her sacred images;

"Here, dear daughter, is the motive that led the Immaculate Heart of Mary to petition Me to ask for this small act of reparation. And, out of regard for her, to move My mercy to pardon those souls who have had the misfortune to offend her. As for you, seek endlessly, with your prayers and sacrifices, to move Me to mercy in regard to these poor souls."

1931, August: Our Lord gives to Sister Lucy in Rianjo, Spain this warning addressed to the Pope and bishops. Jesus says to Sister Lucy: "Make it known to My ministers, given that they follow the example of the King of France in delaying the execution of My command, they will follow him into misfortune."

Remember from above, Our Lord asked the kings of France to consecrate France to His Sacred Heart, they did not, and then one hundred years to the day the masonic revolution stripped the king of power and, four years, later cut off his head. The era of Napoleon followed.

1937, March 19: Pope Pius XI promulgates his encyclical against atheistic Communism. He first explains that he has already condemned Communism in 1924, 1928, 1931, 1932 (twice), and 1933. But it is his solemn duty once more to raise his voice and remind the faithful yet again about the dangers of Communism. Among many other things, the Pope solemnly says: "Communism is intrinsically evil, and no one who would save Christian civilization may collaborate with it in any undertaking whatsoever."

1941: Sister Lucy reveals the first two parts of the Secret in her Memoirs, first on August 31st in her Third Memoir and then again on December 8 in her Fourth Memoir. So, what about that third secret?

1942, October 31 and December 8: Pope Pius XII, acting alone, consecrates the world, but not Russia directly, to the Immaculate Heart of Mary. Our Lord tells Sister Lucy that as a result World War II will be shortened, but that world peace will not result from this consecration.

Before this, the Allies had lost nearly every major battle on land and sea to the Axis, the one exception being Midway in the Pacific. Now, in November, the tide suddenly turned. The Germans are stopped at Stalingrad, suffering their first defeat of the war. At the same time Rommel is finally defeated in Africa at El Alimein. The Americans win their first land battle at Guadalcanal. All of these within weeks of the prayer of Pope Pius XII. Winston Churchill said that it was as if a switch had been flipped. Before this it was always loss after loss, from here on to the end of the war the Allies did not suffer any major loss again. This is the power of the Papacy and prayer.

1944

January 2: Our Lady appears to Sister Lucy and bids her to write down the Third Secret. Our Lady asks it to be revealed to the world not later than 1960. When later asked why the people had to wait for the Third Secret to be revealed in 1960, Sister Lucy states: "Because the Blessed Virgin wishes it so," and, "It [the Third Secret] will be clearer then."

January 9: Sister Lucy commits both texts of the Third Secret to paper by this date.

June 17: The Third Secret is given by Sister Lucy herself to her confessor, Bishop da Silva, since she would not let anyone but a bishop bring it to the Bishop of Fatima.

1952

May: Our Lady appears to Sister Lucy saying: "Make it known to the Holy Father that I am always awaiting the Consecration of Russia to My Immaculate Heart. Without that Consecration, Russia will not be able to convert. Without that Consecration, the world cannot have peace."

July 7: Pope Pius XII consecrates Russia specifically, but he does not ask for the bishops to join him, and thus he is not joined by the Catholic bishops of the world.

September 2: Austrian Jesuit Father Joseph Schweigl is sent by Pope Pius XII to Coimbra, Portugal to interrogate Sister Lucy about the Third Secret. Father Schweigl later confides to one of his colleagues: "I cannot reveal anything of what I learned at Fatima concerning the Third Secret, but I can say that it has two parts: one concerns the Pope. The other, logically — although I must say nothing — would have to be the continuation of the words: In Portugal the dogma of the Faith will always be preserved".

1959, August 17: Pope John XXIII reads the 25-line text of the Third Secret which was taken from the papal apartment and then has his personal secretary, Msgr. Loris Capovilla, write on the envelope: "I leave it to others to comment or decide." The Pope needed a translator due to the difficult dialect. NB- this is the text of the vision.

1960, February 8: As the world anxiously awaits the full revelation of the Third Secret, an unnamed person, who is close to the Pope, authorizes the Press to quote him anonymously that the Third Secret will not be revealed in 1960 and "would probably remain, forever, under absolute seal".

Sister Lucy is officially forbidden to speak about the Third Secret and not allowed to receive any visitors except close relatives and people she has known for a long time. Her own confessor of many years returns from Brazil and is not allowed to see her.

Pope John XXIII reads the 62-line text of the Third Secret, contained in another sealed envelope. Unlike the first text, which he opened in 1959 but could not read without the aid of a translator because of its difficult Portuguese dialect, this text posed no difficulty for the Pope, and he was able to comprehend it completely on his own reading. NB- this is the text of the explanation.

1962, October: Just prior to Vatican Council II, the Vatican Secretariat of State agrees with Moscow that the Council will not condemn Soviet Russia or Communism, in exchange for which two Russian Orthodox observers would attend the Council. This agreement launches the policy of Ostpolitik. This Vatican-Moscow Agreement, which is not allowed by Catholic moral theology (1937), nevertheless is followed, and thus the Vatican Secretariat of State silences those bishops and priests in the Church who are anti-communist at the Second Vatican Council and afterward. Also Vatican II will not make any statements against Communism, despite many bishops' desires.

1963, June 27: Less than a week after becoming pope, Paul VI reads the text of the Third Secret kept in the papal apartment. It is this text— the one which contains Our Lady's words— that is later identified by Cardinal Ottaviani as being 25-lines long.

1964, November 21: At the last day of the third session of the Second Vatican Council, Pope Paul VI consecrates the world to the Immaculate Heart of Mary with no mention of Russia, and the bishops look on but do not join in.

1965, March 27: Pope Paul VI reads the other text of the Third Secret — the one that is 62- lines long. Cardinal Bertone claims that Paul VI read the Third Secret for the first time on this date. However, Archbishop Capovilla testified in his certified note of

May 1967 that Paul VI read the Third Secret for the first time on June 27, 1963.

1967

Sister Lucy's memoirs are published, in which she reveals Our Lady's 1929 request for the Consecration of Russia.

May 13: Sister Lucy meets Pope Paul VI in Fatima and asks him to release the Third Secret, but he refuses.

1978, October 16: Pope John Paul II is elected Pope and reads a text of the Third Secret — the 25-line text that is kept in the papal apartment — within days of his election, according to a statement to Associated Press in May 2000 by his spokesman, Joaquin Navarro-Valls. The statement by Navarro-Valls is contradicted by Msgr. Bertone when he claimed in June 2000 that the Pope first read the Third Secret on July 18, 1981.

1981

May 13: Pope John Paul II is shot and seriously wounded by an assassin.

June 7: The Pope consecrates the world, but not Russia, to the Immaculate Heart of Mary.

July 18: According to Cardinal Bertone, Pope John Paul II reads the Third Secret for the first time. The text he reads is the 62-line text that is kept in the Holy Office archives.

1982

March 21: Sister Lucy informs the Papal Nuncio of the requirements for a valid Consecration of Russia according to the request of Our Lady of Fatima. Sister Lucy's full message is not transmitted to the Pope by the Nuncio. Following the suggestion of Bishop Amaral of Fatima, the Nuncio fails to mention the requirement that the world's bishops participate in the Consecration.

May 12: L'Osservatore Romano, the Pope's own newspaper, publishes an article by Father Umberto Maria Pasquale, S.D.B. (a well-known Salesian priest who has known Sister Lucy since 1939 and had received over 150 letters from her), which reveals that Sister Lucy clearly and emphatically told him that Our Lady of Fatima never asked for the consecration of the world but only the consecration of Russia. Father Pasquale also publishes a photographically-reproduced copy of a handwritten note by Sister Lucy attesting to their conversation on this point.

98

May 13: Pope John Paul II consecrates the world, but not Russia, at Fatima. The bishops of the world do not participate.
1984
March 25: Pope John Paul II, before 250,000 people in Rome, consecrates the world to the Immaculate Heart of Mary. Immediately after he pronounced the words of consecration, he departs from his prepared text and prays, "Enlighten especially the peoples of which You Yourself are awaiting our consecration and confiding". The Pope thus publicly acknowledges that Our Lady of Fatima is still awaiting the Consecration of Russia.

March 26: L'Osservatore Romano reports the exact words spoken by the Holy Father on the 25th.

March 27: The Italian Catholic bishops' newspaper Avvenire reports that the Holy Father, on March 25 at 4:00 in the afternoon, three hours after he consecrated the world, prays at St. Peter's, asking Our Lady to bless "those peoples for whom You Yourself are awaiting our act of consecration and entrusting", and thus again the Pope acknowledges that he did not fulfill Our Lady's request for the Consecration of Russia. The same remarks were reported in L'Osservatore Romano on March 26-27, on page six (Italian edition).

September 10: Bishop Alberto Cosme do Amaral, the Bishop of Fatima, declares during a question and answer session in the aula magna of the Technical University of Vienna, Austria: "Its [the Third Secret's] content concerns only our faith. To identify the Secret with catastrophic announcements or with a nuclear holocaust is to deform the meaning of the message. The loss of faith of a continent is worse than the annihilation of a nation; and it is true that faith is continually diminishing in Europe."

November 11: Jesus magazine publishes an interview with Cardinal Ratzinger. The interview is entitled "Here is Why the Faith is in Crisis" and is published with the Cardinal's explicit permission. Cardinal Ratzinger reveals that he has read the Third Secret and that the Secret refers to "dangers threatening the faith and the life of the Christian, and therefore (the life) of the world". Cardinal Ratzinger says in the same interview that the Secret also refers to "the importance of the Novissimi [the Last Times]", "the absolute importance of history", and that "the things contained in this 'Third Secret 'correspond to what has been announced in Scripture and has been said again and again in many other Marian apparitions, first of all that of Fatima…"

<u>1985, September:</u> In an interview in *Sol de Fatima* magazine, Sister Lucy affirms that the Consecration of Russia still has not been done because Russia was not the clear object of the 1984 consecration, and the world's episcopate did not participate.

<u>1989</u>

<u>July:</u> Father Messias Coelho reveals that Sister Lucy and others have received an anonymous "instruction" from unidentified persons in the Vatican stating that she (and they) must now say that the Consecration of Russia was accomplished on March 25, 1984.

<u>August through November:</u> Five computer-generated and typewritten notes and letters supposedly signed by Sister Lucy suddenly appear, contradicting her previous statements that the Consecration of Russia has not been done. These texts are quickly proven to be fakes, and this fact is published worldwide.

<u>1995:</u> In a personal communication to Professor Baumgartner in Salzburg, Austria, Cardinal Mario Luigi Ciappi — the personal theologian of John Paul II (and of the four popes before him) — reveals that: "In the Third Secret it is foretold, among other things, that the great apostasy in the Church will begin at the top."

<u>1998:</u> Howard Dee, former Philippine ambassador to the Vatican, said in an interview with *Inside the Vatican* magazine that "Bishop Ito [the local bishop of Akita, now deceased] was certain Akita was an extension of Fatima, and Cardinal Ratzinger personally confirmed to me that these two messages, of Fatima and Akita, are essentially the same".

At Akita on October 13, 1973, Our Lady said there would be a worldwide chastisement for sins, in which a great part of humanity would be killed, and that those who survive would envy the dead. (There is a chapter on Akita below)

<u>2000</u>

<u>May 13:</u> At the beatification ceremony of Jacinta and Francisco Marto at Fatima, the Vatican Secretary of State, Cardinal Sodano, announces that the Third Secret of Fatima will be revealed.

<u>June 26:</u> At a press conference, Archbishop Bertone publishes the 62-line text which he claims is the entire Third Secret and also that it refers to the 1981 assassination attempt of John Paul II. The 62-line text describes a vision in which the Pope (a "Bishop dressed in White") is killed by a band of soldiers. This text,

100

containing none of the elements described by Cardinal Ratzinger in his 1984 interview in *Jesus* magazine, is obviously incomplete. Also, Cardinal Bertone claims the Consecration of Russia is done.

2005, February 13: Sister Lucy of Fatima dies less than two months short of her 98th birthday.

2006, November 22: Renowned Italian Catholic commentator and journalist Antonio Socci publishes his book, *The Fourth Secret of Fatima*, which accuses Cardinal Bertone of covering up the complete Third Secret. The book cites the testimony of Archbishop Loris F. Capovilla in July 2006, to Catholic researcher Solideo Paolini, that there are two different texts and two different envelopes pertaining to the Third Secret, that one of the envelopes and its contents — the "Capovilla envelope" — was kept in the papal apartment, not in the archives of the former Holy Office where the text of the vision was lodged, and that Paul VI read its contents on June 27, 1963, two years before the Bertone "official account", which claims that Pope Paul VI first read the text of the Third Secret on March 27, 1965. The "Capovilla envelope" and text have never been produced.

2010

May 11: Pope Benedict XVI, on his pilgrimage to Portugal in May, stunned the press and the Catholic world by saying that the Third Secret of Fatima tells us that "not only from the outside come the attacks against the Pope and the Church, but the sufferings of the Church come from right inside the Church, from the sin that resides inside the Church... we see this today really in a terrifying way: the greatest persecution against the Church doesn't come from its enemies outside, but starts from the sins within the Church".

May 13: Before 500,000 pilgrims, the Pope proclaimed (in reference to the Third Secret): "Whoever thinks that the prophetic mission of Fatima is concluded deceives himself."

The rest of this chapter will briefly look at some possible insights into what is said in the explanation of the third secret. Here I will point out that I take for granted the explanation is part of the secret, and that it has not been revealed.

POPE JOHN PAUL II IN FULDA, GERMANY (1980)

Published Testimony:

The October 1981 issue of the German magazine *Stimme des Glaubens* reported on a discussion that Pope John Paul II had with a select group of German Catholics, in November of 1980. The following is a verbatim report of the discussion:

Text of the Published Report:

The Holy Father was asked, "What about the Third Secret of Fatima? Should it not have already been published by 1960?"

Pope John Paul II replied: "Given the seriousness of the contents, my predecessors in the Petrine office diplomatically preferred to postpone publication so as not to encourage the world power of Communism to make certain moves.

"On the other hand, it should be sufficient for all Christians to know this: if there is a message in which it is written that the oceans will flood whole areas of the earth, and that from one moment to the next millions of people will perish, truly the publication of such a message is no longer something to be so much desired."

The Pope continued: "Many wish to know simply from curiosity and a taste for the sensational, but they forget that knowledge also implies responsibility. They only seek the satisfaction of their curiosity, and that is dangerous if at the same time they are not disposed to do something, and if they are convinced that it is impossible to do anything against evil."

At this point the Pope grasped a Rosary and said: "Here is the remedy against this evil. Pray, pray, and ask for nothing more. Leave everything else to the Mother of God."

The Holy Father was then asked: "What is going to happen to the Church?"

He answered: "We must prepare ourselves to suffer great trials before long, such as will demand of us a disposition to give up even life, and a total dedication to Christ and for Christ... With your and my prayer it is possible to mitigate this tribulation, but it is no longer possible to avert it, because only thus can the Church be effectively renewed. How many times has the renewal of the Church sprung from blood! This time, too, it will not be otherwise. We must be strong and prepared, and trust in Christ and His Mother, and be very, very assiduous in praying the Rosary."

102

Commentary

I would like to note here that the above comments on the vision which is part of the Third Secret were intentionally made without reference to these comments. I knew about these comments before I wrote my own comments above.

Let's get into this. The Pope mentions first the reason, or at least a reason, that the secret was not revealed, namely a fear about possible reactions by the communists. I'm struck by this fear and instantly think of the words of the Lord, "And fear ye not them that kill the body, and are not able to kill the soul: but rather fear him that can destroy both soul and body in hell." Mk 10:28

The Pope then gives an insight into what is contained in the message referring to the material chastisement. NB- Fatima scholars, indeed anyone who studies Divine Chastisements, usually make a distinction between the spiritual and material chastisement. Hence the quote from St. Mark. Here he references some aspects of the material chastisement. Namely, that there will be flooding of "whole areas of the earth, and that from one moment to the next millions of people will perish". Clearly, unless the communists have developed super weapons we are unaware of, these actions are from God who is the only one with that kind of power. This being the case, why, "truly the publication of such a message is no longer something to be so much desired?" I should think any father would want to warn his children of impending doom.

The Pope goes on to speak of the responsibility that always comes with knowledge. I think most can readily accept that, but why prejudge all peoples as simply seeking the sensational out of the sin of curiosity? Curiosity is the sin by which someone seeks to know something that does not pertain to their station in life. For example a layman, who is clearly not and never could be an exorcist, studying books about the demonic and possession. But here, knowledge of worldwide catastrophes is clearly within the realm of everyone on the Earth where these events could take place. He continues by saying this knowledge is useless if people think they cannot do anything against evil. I immediately think of the Prophet Jonah who is tasked by God to go to Nineveh and call the people to repentance with the warning that if they do not, God will chastise them by destroying their city. They repent and save the city. What would happen if people were told by the Pope of a much greater chastisement? Why would people today not repent? He concludes this line of thought with a call to praying the Rosary, while asking for nothing, thus trusting in Our Lady. This is what Our Lady asked for at Fatima.

Responding to a question about the future of the Church, the Pope references another probable aspect of the still hidden Third Secret. Namely that the Church will suffer great persecution and even many Catholics will be killed. Thus the call to be ready to die for Christ. He then concludes with an ominous warning that the above mentioned chastisements cannot be avoided. All that we can do now is to mitigate, or lessen, the effects of them. Also he speaks of a renewal in the Church. This is quite a statement by itself because he is speaking in 1980, now fifteen years into the "renewal" of Vatican II. It seems here that he is at least implying that all the changes and "renewal" that had been going on, are not the actual renewal at all. The actual renewal will only happen after these terrible events. Maybe three quarters of the people on Earth are wiped out in an instant? That has not happened...yet. Further, he says that the blood of the faithful is the source of renewal. This is an age old theme in Christianity, the blood of the martyrs. He ends with a call for hope, strong faith, trust in Christ and Our Lady, and finally another call to pray the Rosary.

This statement leaves me absolutely dumbfounded. The Pope clearly knew that Our Lady had warned, in 1917, of impending doom if she was not obeyed. Yet we have seen seven Popes come and go without a simple prayer of consecration for Russia, let alone at least seventy years without telling the good People of God what is in the Third Secret. Why are they so afraid? Don't they believe that the King of the Universe who is the Savior of the World can protect them and us? Do they not realize that Our Queen only desires our salvation and that all of this is for our good? In any event Our Lady, while not being heeded, yet, revealed at another apparition, this time in Japan, some of the hidden message of the Third Secret. I have a chapter on Our Lady of Akita, later in the book.

Prayers given by the Angel of Peace in preparation for the apparitions:

"My God, I believe, I adore, I hope, and I love Thee. I ask pardon for all those who do not believe in Thee, do not adore Thee, do not hope in Thee, do not love Thee." Said three times while kneeling in reparation for those who do not believe, adore, hope in, or love God.

"Most Holy Trinity, Father, Son, and Holy Ghost, I adore Thee profoundly, and I offer Thee the Most Precious Body, Blood, Soul, and Divinity of the same Son, Jesus Christ, present in the Tabernacles of the world, in reparation for all the sacrileges, outrages and indifferences by which He Himself is offended. And by the infinite merits of His Most Sacred Heart and through the Immaculate Heart of Mary, I beg of Thee the conversion of poor sinners." Said three times while prostrate on the ground.

These two prayers, given by the Angel of peace, are highly recommended. I would add that this second prayer is very efficacious especially when it is said with piety during the elevation of the chalice at the Sacrifice of the Mass, or even in the presence of the Most Blessed Sacrament outside of mass. Of course at Mass it should be said mentally so as not to disturb the other faithful.

Our Lady asked that the children and by extension everyone to pray the Rosary daily, inserting the following prayer after each decade;"O my Jesus, forgive us our sins, save us from the fires of Hell, lead all souls to Heaven, especially those most in need."(Many add here "of Thy mercy")

In the next chapter, we shall answer the question, "Did we listen well to Our Lady?" If she came to offer an end to WWI, the most obvious evidence is WWII, which means we did not listen to Her.

Chapter 8
How did we get here? Part Five
From the Peace at Versailles to the bombing of everyone

In this chapter we will look at the time bomb that is commonly called the Peace of Versailles all the way through WWII. These were the violent consequences of the ideas developed in the 19th, which Our Lady has never stopped warning us about.

<u>A handful of heretical priests can really do a number</u>
Jesuit priest Pierre Teilhard de Chardin (1881- 1955), who is said to be the father of the "new age", is often noted as the most influential figure in the pantheistic and eclectic movement. Devoted to evolution, he embraced an evolutionary Pantheism. In *Christianity and Evolution*, he wrote, "the biological process now taking place in mankind consists…in the progressive development of a collective human consciousness. And…I can only be saved only [sic] by becoming one with the universe. Thereby, to, my deepest 'pantheist' aspiration are [sic] satisfied…A religion of evolution: that, when all is said and done, is what Man needs ever more explicitly if he is to survive and 'super-live'…the comparative value of religious creeds may be measured by their respective power of evolutive activation…Man's origin by way of evolution is now an indubitable fact for science. There can be no two ways about it… to continue to debate it in schools… is a waste of time. Is evolution a theory, a system, or a hypothesis? It is much more: it is a general condition to which all theories, all hypotheses, all systems must bow and which they must satisfy henceforward if thereby be thinkable and true. Evolution is a light illuminating all facts, a curve that all lines must follow."[xix]
Thus, Teilhard demands that evolution is a first principle that cannot be questioned. He wanted to combine all religions into one. In 1957, the Holy Office ordered his works to be removed from the Catholic world, 1962 the Holy Office warned that his works were filled with ambiguities and serious errors counter to the faith, these were repeated in 1981. How did a Jesuit come to this? He wrote that he was visited in his dreams by a spirit that took possession of him. In *The Heart of the Matter* he wrote that at a young age he was fascinated with matter, at age 10 his interests were in "a

continued and increased contact with the Cosmic 'in the solid state'". As a young man he hit "a standstill in the 'awaking of Cosmic Life'". And required "the intervention of a new force or a new illumination... For, if the initial call that I had heard was in fact coming from Matter, then (someone kept whispering within me) why should I not look for the essence of Matter, for its 'heart'?". He discovered "a presence... the consciousness of a deep-running, ontological, total Current which embraced the whole Universe... this consciousness... filled the whole horizon of my inner being... and that fire had been kindled...[through] the cult of Matter, the cult of Life, and the cult of Energy." In *The Spiritual Power of Matter* he recalls this account from 1919, "express more successfully than I could today the heady emotion I experienced at that time from my contact with Matter". Writing in the third person, he recounts his interaction with a being he calls "the thing", "the man was walking in the desert when 'the thing' swooped down on him. Then suddenly a breath of scorching air passed across his forehead, broke through the barrier of his closed eyelids, and penetrated his soul. The man felt he was ceasing to be merely himself. An irresistible rapture took possession of him as though all the sap of all living things was mightily refashioning in feeble fibers of his being. At the same time the anguish of some superhuman peril oppressed him. A confessed feeling of the force that had swept down upon him was equivocal, turbid, the combined essence of all evil, all goodness." Then 'the thing' said, "You called me, here I am. Grown weary of abstractions, attenuations, the wordiness of social life [sic]. You wanted to put yourself against reality entire and untamed. I was waiting for you in order to be made holy, and now I'm established on you for life or for death. He who has once seen me can never forget me. He must either damn himself with me, or save me with himself." Clearly this was a preternatural experience. It is very similar to the episode that Descartes experienced.

In the 1936 *The Great Heresies*, Hilaire Bellock wrote, "the new advance against the Church— what will perhaps prove the final advance against the Church, what is at any rate the only modern enemy of consequence— is fundamentally Materialist.... [it] regards man as sufficient to himself... and— the fundamental point— God as no more than a figment of the imagination...whereas the denial of God had been confined in the past to a comparatively small number of intellectuals, that denial has now gained the multitude and is acting everywhere as a social force. This is the modern enemy: this is that rising flood; the greatest and what may prove to be the final struggle between the Church and the world. The Modern Attack advanced so far that... of two things one must happen... Either the Catholic Church... will be reduced by her modern enemies... to silence; or the Catholic Church will... recover and restore the world... The Modern Attack is so universal and moving so rapidly that men now very young will surely live to see something like a decision in this great battle. "[xx]

It would be good to recall the Papal clarifications in those years relative to the Sacred Texts: *Dei Filius, Providentissimus Deus, Pascendi Dominici Gregis, Spiritus Paraclitus, Divino Afflante Spiritu, Humani Generis.* When read together it is quite clear that the Sacred Scriptures are: inspired, inerrant, truthful, and, at the same time, must be read within the context of Sacred Tradition in union with the living and true Magisterium. Sadly many Catholics, even clerics, do not follow the clear directives of the Church and come up with nonsensical interpretations. For example, they may say the great flood was not worldwide but local, or that the miracle of the loaves was not multiplication but sharing. The list is long and sorrowful.

As we have seen thus far, the erroneous ideas of Nominalism, Materialism, Rationalism, and Romanticism have real effects in society. The occupants of the Petrine Office were not ignorant of this. One of the important writings on society is *Rerum Novarum*, by Pope Leo XIII, in 1891. This seminal work on modern Catholic social thought addresses the plight of the industrial workers in the wake of the Industrial Revolution. It calls for the protection of the weak and the poor through the pursuit of justice while excluding Socialism and class struggle as illegitimate principles of change. It affirms the dignity of work, the right to private property, and the right to form and join professional associations. *Quadragesimo Anno* (After Forty Years) by Pope Pius XI, in 1931, was written in response to the alarming concentration of wealth and power in the socio-economic realm, and it calls for the reestablishment of a social order based on the principle of subsidiarity. In commemorating the 40th anniversary of *Rerum Novarum*, this encyclical reaffirms the need for a social order animated by justice.

108

Pacem in Terris (Peace on Earth) by Pope John XXIII, in 1963, covers the entire spectrum of relations between individuals, between the individual and the community, and between nations. John XXIII affirms the inviolability of human rights. Peace, based on mutual trust, can be well-founded only if undergirded by a unity of right order in human affairs arising from a genuine respect for and adherence to the law of God.

You were called to prayer, penance, conversion, but you wanted more war

We were warned by Our Lady that if people did not repent and stop offending God, then a worse war, worse than WWI, would be launched. It is good to remember that war is a chastisement for sin. Even a cursory glance at war reveals that, "war is hell". It is not just the obvious effects of war— the destruction of entire cities, peoples, and nations physically— but the immediate and enduring effects on the people involved. Think about how man has a natural aversion to killing other men. Somehow he has to overcome this tendency to become effective in combat. A study I read some years ago revealed that in the US Civil War 10% of the soldiers shot to kill on their first day of combat. By WWI this had arisen to about 25%, by WWII 50%, and Vietnam 75%. This leaves a kind of scar on the interior life of everyone, independent of surviving the war or not. One simply cannot be taken from normal life, having little inclination to kill another, and then only months later, be trained and willing to do just that without incurring major interior harm.

Obviously the loss of life, especially as most of the combatants are relatively young, is yet another wound with which family, friends, and communities are left to reckon. How many great men and women lost their lives too early, before they could fulfill the plan that God had ordained for them?

I am left wondering what the world would be like today if the call to prayer and penance had been heeded. While it is undeniable that people of goodwill did pray and do penance, many did not. We know this because WWII happened with all its terrible results. On the other hand, it is an oft-repeated maxim that "there are no atheists in fox holes". Certainly many that saw the terrors of war also found the consolation of Christ. We can look at the relative rise of religious participation during and after the war. But just as these rose during WWI, and fell away, so too they rose and fell away after WWII, so that, as the 50's were coming to an end, the gains of religious activity were almost at the pre-war level.

Total war, not a new idea, but with bigger toys

The concept of Total War has been said to have been fully realized in WWII. What is Total War? Your enemy encompasses all of the people and objects related to your antagonist, and thus everything is open to destruction. In contrast, for millennia, the accepted sphere of war encompassed only the soldiers and their immediate supplies. It was considered unjust to intentionally target "non-combatants" in any military operation. That is not to say that non-combatants and their property were always exempt from the effects of any given battle, but they were not "targeted" as such. Total War makes very little distinction. For example, a major complaint in the colonies was the unlawful requirement to house and feed the soldiers of the King of England, a justification for the American Revolution. Napoleon had no qualms, when needed, to take the food of locals when his supplies ran low. This mindset was emulated by Sherman in the American Civil War, and expanded to include destroying farms, fields, and livestock to starve the South into submission. This was broadened slightly during WWI with a small number of activities that intentionally targeted heavily civilian-occupied areas with the aim of harming the armies of the enemy. While these actions did kill civilians and destroy some building and railways, they had little real effect on the outcome of the war.

With the rise of the modern means of war— planes, tanks, rockets, and more— the possibility of even greater destruction should have made the military leaders more circumspect in their tactics. However, the tide of Total War only rose higher when all sides of WWII used these more efficient means of destruction to target even more civilians. The justification adopted, and often repeated, is that in the end it is alright to destroy cities of the enemy because it will cause them to lose the "will to fight". Many studies of this strategy have shown the opposite to be true. Not only did the wanton killing of civilians far behind the front line not deteriorate the *esprit de corps*", but it actually made all the nations which endured it fight harder.

Let us think of the "fire bombing" of Dresden, Germany, a classic city of highly talented wood-workers and carvers. To argue that it had a military advantage against Germany is mindboggling. Yet it was burned and a couple hundred thousand, mostly women, children, and old men, (because the fighting-age men were on the fronts) died in a fire that could be seen hundreds of miles away. To this we can add the same situation in multiple cities in Japan that had one or two, if that, military factories, as well as the needless bombing of London which we would be remiss not to mention. The result of which was no discernible impact on the war, other than to harden the English into fighting better and enduring more. Finally, they say the bombing of Hiroshima and Nagasaki were justified because it forced the Japanese Empire to surrender. However, there is good evidence that Japan was about to surrender anyway and that the A-bombs almost pushed them to fight on, given the barbarity of their application. And besides, we are never allowed to commit a bad act for a good end. How can one defend the wholesale destruction of an entire city in an instant?

Possible reasons for crimes against humanity?

The simple truth is that Total War, or in any event, war as it has devolved in the past century, has resulted in wholesale crimes against humanity. While it is true that camps of the Nazis, as horrible as they were, should be exposed and abhorred, the fact is that all of the main combatants during WWII had camps of "detainees". NB- The Russian, German, and Japanese "camps" caused the largest loss of life. Were any of them just or legal? Of course, every country that had a camp also had "legal" justifications for them, but not legal in the sense that they were in conformity with Divine Law. Can a country detain people in their own lands which they determine to be antithetical to the state, even though they have not broken any just laws? Just because someone is of Japanese origin, it seems unjust to put them in a prison camp for years out of a fear of a possible future crime. The same goes for Jews, Catholics, or anyone.

It has been argued that the so called "strategic bombings" of WWII were a necessary part of the war and resulted in the ultimate victory of the Allies. This seems improbable at best. First of all, the majority of the fighting in Europe was between the Germans and Russians. Neither side had any significant ability to mass bomb each other. In reality the Russians beat the Germans, and, even if the Americans and British never fought the Germans, Russia probably would have won anyway. In the Pacific, one of the main factors that led the Japanese to surrender was the lack of resources, food, gasoline, ammunition, and other materials. This, however, was due mainly to the naval blockade, in large part accomplished by the stunning work of the US submarine fleet, not by the wanton burning of Japanese cities. While the bombing of both German and Japanese factories slowed their manufacturing capabilities, they never stopped, and the results on the actual, front-line soldiers were minimal if not nonexistent.

I bring up these aspects of war simply to point out that modern war, as with so many other aspects of life, has far too often treated the inherent worth of a man— due to the fact that he is made in the image and likeness of God— as little more than a cog in a machine. This applies to the treatment of both allies and foes.

The other reason I have brought up these aspects of war is to bring into focus a larger question. Why does the good God allow us to make war with each other, and what is He trying to teach us?

One lesson that I think should come from reflecting on the hell of war is that in the midst of these terrors, the characteristics and aspects of man make us far more similar than different. In the end, we will all die, and we are all brothers and sisters in this human family. It is always sad to see families fight and most sad to see nations fight.

In studying and reflecting on the world wars, the reality is that there were no true winners, only varying degrees of losers. When victory was "announced", almost immediately, the charade of allegiance and friendship revealed itself to be just that, a charade. I'm not saying that there is a natural animosity between the atheistic regime of the communists and the, at least on paper, freedom of the "West", but rather that while the large battles and the like came to an end, an immediate and much deadlier war started. Deadlier here is used to point out the reality that when this "Cold War" started there was a clear ideological divide between the atheistic, man-centered, and the western, God is acceptable, sides of the argument. That was then. Now, however, both sides seem to have replaced God with man.

Chapter 9
How did we get here? Part Six
From "Post War" To Vatican II

In this chapter, we will look at the period following the "official" end of WWII to the start of the Second Vatican Council. I used quotations for the title of post war because the war did not really end, it only became the "Cold War". First, we will see how quickly the eugenicists adjust to the tides of popular opinion. By "adjust", I mean that they adjusted their wording, while incorporating the same tactics, and were so effective that they rewrote the laws. They then glory over the death of Christian ideals in the US, while the US never stops claiming to be Christian, and turn their sights on the Church. Modernism begins to reign.

<u>Now that the war is over, let's get back to killing babies and sterilization</u>
In the wake of WWII, revelations of the forced work camps and "death" camps of the Nazi regime began. Needless to say, the peoples of the West were horrified. This had a secondary effect of justifying the war and actions of the Allies against the Nazis and the German people they ruled. Let me be clear here, the basic reason for the war in Europe to "free" the people that had been overrun and to keep England free are legitimate reasons for the war. However, while there were some in leadership that knew of the actions in these "camps", most of the public, and indeed most of the soldiers and airmen, did not know until just before the end of the war or just after the completion.

Nevertheless, the reality of the atrocities of the war and the reasoning behind them, were shocking. People became very sensitive against any justification for the killing of the innocent, forced sterilization, and the like. Thus the people in the West that were on board with these actions had to come up with a new plan. After all, they certainly didn't want people to know that Hitler said he got his ideas for population control from the eugenicists in the USA and England. Thus, for a decade, the population control people had to stay out of sight, out of mind, and let the horrors of war and so forth die down. But they didn't stay inactive for long.

In 1956, the eugenics people gathered in London to restart with new ideas. Frederick Osborn proposed a change in strategy: "Let's stop telling everyone that they have a generally inferior genetic quality, for they will never agree. Let's base our proposals on the desirability of having children born in homes where they will get affectionate and responsible care, and perhaps our proposals will be accepted."

Thus the eugenic societies went crypto. The term eugenics faded and the term "social biology" came into fashion. Now becoming free from being linked to the horrors of the Nazis, they moved on to push contraception and abortion. In 1959 the American eugenics groups decided to redefine pregnancy so as to make the murder of babies more acceptable. Thus the "implantation of a fertilized embryo" not the fertilization itself should mark the beginning of pregnancy. It was stated, "The social advantage of being considered to prevent conception rather than to destroy an established pregnancy could depend on something so simple as a prudent habit of speech." In 1963, Garret Harden wrote, "Murder by definition, is the unlawful killing... we can define murder any way we want to. How do we want to define it? ... where do we draw the line?... most societies... draw it very late— some hours or days after birth... before this, the infant is not a member of the community, and killing it is permitted... Whether the fetus is or is not a human being is a matter of definition... it would be unwise to define the fetus as human... [given our belief that] the early fetus may, with [freedom], be flushed down the toilet or thrown out with the garbage...."

It would be good to reflect that when the baby-killers started to redefine and thus make people rethink their concepts on mothers and babies, nearly everyone in the Western World thought that a new baby was present at the moment of conception. One must ask, was this wrong? Can we now say that those people back then simply had a limited "scientific" understanding, and we now have a more developed and mature understanding of the "science"? More to the point, has the "science" changed? Certainly the biology hasn't. One can't really argue that women are different today than say fifty years ago, and neither are babies. So what has changed?

The concepts put forward by the baby-killers have worked. You could even say that they have worked quite remarkably. Look at the fact that even most pro-baby people use the term fetus,

which can be defined as an unborn offspring of a mammal. If now
an unborn baby is just an unborn mammal, why not kill it? Besides
this, they were successful in changing the laws to allow for legal
killings. The term abortion is another example of a "sterilization of
terms". Of course abortion is not as nasty a word as, "killing a
baby," even though they mean the same thing. The plan to land
men on the moon in the Apollo XIII mission was aborted, but I'm
quite sure the result was not the death of a little child.

Remember as has been noted earlier, the concepts of
Nominalism and legal Positivism generally state that a rule or law
is good, simply because it is a rule or law given by a legitimate
authority. This was the justification for Anglicanism, the Great
Schism, and indeed every schism from the Church. Thus, we have
seen that many people make moral judgments based on the law, not
on morality. In other words, if it is legal, then it must be okay.
People do this all the time. In the 1950's divorce was legally very
difficult to do and costly, but now there is "no-fault divorce" which
is very cheap and easy. Thus, when it was hard and costly, there
were few divorces. Now that it is cheap and easy, half of marriages
end in divorce.

When it comes to divorce or the killing of babies, the law is
not the arbiter of morality. God is the judge and arbiter of morality.
Law, good and just laws, are required to follow Divine Law. In
these cases they clearly do not. Ideas have consequences.

Good plan, but we need it in writing, and by that I mean change the laws

In 1962, the American Law Institute joined with the eugenics
movement to target abortion laws with its "Model Penal Code",
that is, a collection of suggested legal guidelines for state
legislatures that pressed for a change in abortion laws. Using the
new re-definition of pregnancy, they wanted "drugs or other
substances for avoiding pregnancy, whether by preventing
implantation of a fertilized ovum or by any other method that
operates before, at or immediately after fertilization". Also they
argued for "justified abortion": "A licensed physician is justified in
terminating a pregnancy if he believes there is a substantial risk
that continuance of the pregnancy would gravely impair the
physical or mental health of the mother, or that the child would be

born with grave physical or mental defects, or that the pregnancy resulted from rape, incest, or other felonious intercourse."

In 1965, the contrived case *Griswold vs Connecticut* made all forms of contraception legal by fiat of the Supreme Court. In 1967, California, Colorado, and North Carolina changed their laws to conform to the "Model Penal Code". By 1972, abortions were up to over 100,000 annually in California. In 1969, Planned Parenthood made public its long standing support of abortion on demand and came up with a plan for the government to pay for abortion, contraception, and sterilization. They wanted to tax married people more than singles, and an extra tax on married couples with more than two children in school. Also, they wanted to restructure the family, promote homosexuality, and put contraceptive drugs in the water supply. In 1973, *Roe vs. Wade* legalized abortion nationwide. It is estimated that 1.5 Billion children have been aborted worldwide since 1980. These numbers make the communist and fascist death camps look like child's play.

With the above ideas in mind, we can see the effects of many simply using the "legality" of an act as the determining factor for the "justness" of an act. This is, of course, a bit of a head-scratcher, especially for the people alive in the 50's and 60's, because they had just witnessed a hated regime (Nazis) that had made and passed laws giving them the legal "rights" to do exactly what they did. Why did more people not raise an objection to the "change of laws"?

The ideas which we have covered in previous chapters now show their fruits. The effects of Rationalism, in which man is judge of truth; Materialism, in which the only thing that actually exists is the physical world; Romanticism, the separation of faith and reason and subordination of faith to reason; and Imminentism, in which the individual is the judge of the true, good, and beautiful; have all led to the "dictatorship of Relativism". This dictatorship will not allow the objective truth to slow down or change its ultimate goal: the destruction of objective reality. The main bulwark and proponent of reality is the Church, thus the Church must go.

I know we put "in God we trust" on the dollar, but really...

How could a "Christian" nation, as many have claimed the US to be in its very founding and basis of laws, yet make abortion legal? St. Thomas taught in the Summa, Part II, Q93, A. 3, "since then the eternal law is the plan of government in the Chief

Governor, all the plans of government in the inferior governors must be derived from the eternal law… all laws, in so far as they partake of right reason, are derived from the eternal law". Yet we have *Everson vs. Board of Education*'s 1947 adoption of the separation of Church and State; *Engel vs. Vitale* in 1962 saying prayer in public school is unconstitutional; *Reed vs. Van Hoven* in 1965 making it unconstitutional for kids to pray aloud over lunch; *Roe vs. Wade* in 1973 legalizing the killing of babies; *Lawrence vs. Texas* in 2003 legalizing homosexual sodomy, and to this Justice Scalia dissented, "marked the end of all moral legislation" and observed that "the Court has taken sides in the culture war". He also predicted, "The Court today pretends… that we need not fear judicial imposition of homosexual marriage… do not believe it." *Obergefell vs Hodges* in 2015 legalized homosexual unions. Clearly these "judicial laws" do not derive from the eternal law.

It is interesting that one of the early strategies in the "Cold War" was to mark the differences between the Christian West and the atheistic communists by highlighting that the West had a "trust in God". This statement was thought to be so important as a defense against the spread of Communism, that it was placed on the currency of the USA in 1956. Yet as we have seen in the above paragraph, the courts do not seem to be following the claims of that statement.

Here I do not want to get into the discussion of the courts effectively making laws, an obligation and privilege that seems to be the prerogative of the legislative branch. Rather, I want to simply note that if it's the case that a proper defense of Western society also means a defense of the fundamental ideas that make up that society, then we are witnessing a slow yet consistent revolution from within. Also while I use court decisions in the US, this and similar actions to "legalize" that which clearly goes against the eternal law, has been repeated quite thoroughly throughout the Western World. The point is, many in public will state that they believe in God and still work for the opposite goals. This is only possible because many, or most, have embraced the irrational thinking of the previously mentioned philosophers.

Looks like our friends have finished off Christendom, let's get the Church

By the time the 1950's came around the ideas of the rationalist had advanced into the Church even further. Of course there were and are holy people that truly believed, but confusion and obfuscation were taking over. This is the atmosphere in which the second Vatican council was started and finished . At the end of the council, Paul VI declared that the council did not teach anything definitively, that it was merely "pastoral". If that is true, I concede this point is contentious, then the "pastoral suggestions" and so forth can be taken or left. Further, if this council was pastoral, which is defined as a way of Priestly ministry, then why is it treated so rigidly as the only way of spreading the Gospel and saving souls?

The misplaced ideas of the philosophers that have been put forward thus far can be summed up with the title of Modernism, as a category for those that adhere to them within the Church. This is the name, or category of peoples, that has been used by the popes, so I will stick with it. I would like to point out that ideas of the modernists, which is those within the Church, are so in line with the same ideas of the secularists outside the Church, it is often impossible to see any difference. Of course, the reason is that there is no difference. The only real difference is that those in the Church try to remake theology in order to remake the faith. Those outside the Church try to remake laws, thinking, and rhetoric to remake society. The goal is the same for both, the destruction of objective reality so that man can do whatever he wants. Or to state it a little more forcefully, to replace God with Man, to ignore that God is the King of the World and any authority to govern is granted by Him. Thus with this goal in mind the modernists infiltrated into the very heart of the Church..

In the next chapter, with the world embroiled in the consequences of heretical ideas, and the Church infiltrated thoroughly by Modernism, we will look at the Second Vatican Council, occurring at this time.

Chapter 10
Results of the "Aggiornamento" vs. the Principle of the Excluded Middle

In this chapter we will look at the results of Vatican II. The details of the time from when John XXIII called for a council until its end have been thoroughly covered in many books. I will not go over all the details here. Instead I will look at some insights given in the years immediately after the council and then the results of the council in our present time, more than fifty years later. The exposition of the results, the effects, will primarily be by way of statistics. But I will also add some of my own reflections because my life in the Church started a little more than a decade after the close of the council. Finally, we will have to come to some conclusions about the state of the Church today. Simply put, are we in a crisis? Is this crisis due to the council? And what are the results of the philosophical principals that we have been looking at in this book, namely the collection of them that is called "Modernism"?

The Third Secret is not Important
On August 17, 1959, Pope John XXIII read the first part of the Third Secret and said, "I will leave it to others to comment or decide." On February 8, 1960, the Pope read the longer part of the Third Secret, and the Vatican— through an unnamed person— released to the press that the secret would not be released in 1960 and would probably never be released. It was also suggested by those close to the Pope that he stated that the Third Secret "did not pertain to his papacy". In any event, he clearly decided the secret was not important enough to be reveal. However, as we will see, he did not leave it alone.

On October 11, 1962, Pope John XXIII officially started the Second Vatican Council with an address to more than 3,500 Bishops gathered in St. Peter's Basilica on Vatican Hill in Rome. In these opening remarks he stated:

"In the daily exercise of Our pastoral ministry, sometimes come to our ears, hurting them, certain insinuations of some people who, even in their ardent zeal, lack the sense of discretion and measure. They do not see in modern times but prevarication and ruin; they are saying that our time, compared with the past, has been getting worse; and behave as if they had learned nothing from history, that remains a teacher of life, and as if in the time of the preceding Ecumenical Councils everything had proceeded with an absolute triumph of doctrine and Christian life, and of the just freedom of the Church.

"It seems fair to Us to disagree with such prophets of calamities, trained to announce always unfortunate events, as if the end of time were imminent. In the present historical moment, Providence is taking us to a new order of human relations that, by the very work of men but even more above their own intentions, are directed towards the fulfillment of superior and unexpected plans; for everything, even the human adversities, it arranges for the greater good of the Church."

It would be good to note here that the Pope references those who say the modern world is getting worse and that in modern times there were no problems in doctrine, morals, or the freedoms of the Church. He goes on to openly disagree with the "prophets of calamities" (other translations have it as "prophets of doom"). Most of the commentators on this point agree that John XXIII is referring here to the children of Fatima, but one could also include any or all of the past Marian Apparitions that warn of a future chastisement as well as the many mystics that had predicted the same. It is also quite ominous that he next mentions "a new order of human relations" that will come about by the work of man, but will fulfill superior and unknown plans, and that this will somehow result in a benefit for the Church. It seems as if he is saying the plans of secret societies will work out for the good of everyone.

In these brief sentences at the heart of his address, he ridicules those that warn of the downward trend of society, even the supernatural interventions of Our Lady, (on the very Feast of the Motherhood of God), and says that secret or "unexpected" plans, "superior" plans, will be good. He is also here directly disagreeing with his predecessor, Pope St. Pius X, and his immediate predecessor, Pope Pius XII, both of whom stated that the times they were living in were the worst times in human history. Thus, these two Popes when seen side by side were saying together that things are terrible and getting worse. This is of course not dependent on Papal Infallibility, nor does it require a great deal of insight, only a little reflection on history and an observant mind. Anyone would have to be nearly completely ignorant of the past to not join in this simple, albeit dire, observation. Or we all could simply choose to live in fantasy land where everything is creampuffs and lollypops. Nevertheless, not only did John XXIII not obey a simple request from Our Lady, and reiterated by Our Lord (the requests of the apparitions), he goes on to downplay the message by saying they "lack the sense of discretion and measure". He doesn't believe the message came from heaven.

I thought you opened the window to let in fresh air, now the smoke of Satan is in

The so called "*aggiornamento*" (Italian) of Vatican II was supposed to be an "updating". This was the main purpose that Pope John XIII gave for Vatican II. He explained further that the implementation of the idea could be seen as a kind of "opening up of the windows" of the Church to the modern world. In one sense it can be understood to be an enticing proposition. If we look at the general historic situation of the 1950's, one can easily see an ever-widening gap between the teachings, and thus morals, of the Church with the rest of the West. Of course, this was in large part due to the destruction of Christendom and the secularization and liberalization of the Western World. It was not so much that the Church changed, quite the opposite, but rather that the previously Christian societies had left the Church. We can understand why it might seem a good idea to open up the windows as it were and update the Church. On the other hand, with hindsight, it is quite clear that when the windows were opened, smoke came in.

From June 21, 1963 to his death on August 6, 1978, Pope Paul VI was the Vicar of Christ on Earth. During these fifteen years he oversaw the majority of Vatican II, introduced a New Mass called the *Novus Ordo*, and suppressed the Traditional Mass and Rites of the Church. Thus he replaced not just the Mass but all the Rites (Baptism, Confirmation, Ordination, Eucharist, Marriage, Confession, Extreme Unction, Blessings, Exorcism, and more). Needless to say, all these changes had a profound effect on the life of the Church. We will go over some statistics later in this chapter.

It seems clear from interviews, statements and so forth, that Pope Paul VI started his reign very optimistically. Why not? He was in good health, the Church was in good health, and she was growing. The missions were doing well, and this great council had just started. However, within ten years he seems to have had a major change of mind. He wrote in a letter, June 29, 1972;

> "We would say that, through some mysterious crack— no, it's not mysterious; through some crack, the smoke of Satan has entered the Church of God. There is doubt, uncertainty, problems, unrest, dissatisfaction, confrontation. The Church is no longer trusted. We trust the first pagan prophet we see who speaks to us in some newspaper, and we run behind him and ask him if he has the formula for true life. I repeat, doubt has entered our conscience. And it entered through the windows that should have been open to the light: science."[xxi]

What is the "smoke of Satan" to which he is referring? Could it be that the smell of the *Novus Ordo* is not so sweet? Could it be that "updating" everything in the life of the Church was already starting to have horrible consequences? We know now that the abuse of children was widespread as well as the homosexual predation of clerics. Not to mention, the huge drop in vocations, the large number of clerics and religious abandoning their vocations.

In any event, even as early as the middle of '72 just seven years after the close of the council, and only two and half years after the introduction of a totally new mass, Paul VI saw the smoke of Satan. He also realized that people were turning away from the true Church and were turning to the Neo-Paganism of modern mass media and thought. He seems to have realized that the idea that "science" had the answers was just another empty promise. At this point in his life he must have felt stuck. What could he do? He had just been the architect of the biggest changes in the two thousand year history of the Church. Clearly he couldn't just go back to way things were and say this "experiment" has failed. In fact, even as he seems to see to failures of the changes, he didn't do anything to fix what he had torn down.

Statistics say the faith is losing

We will now look at a few statistics so that we can see the objective reality of the results of Vatican II. I think it is fitting to look at statistics for a of couple reasons: first, the numbers are just that, numbers. They can't honestly be argued with, and they show reality as it actually is. Second, many, if not all, of the changes were proposed as experiments. When the good and faithful Catholics were told that all these things were changing they were often also told, this is what the Holy Father wants and these are just experiments; they may not last, so just try it out. Let's look at how the "experiments" turned out. NB- For simplicity we will look here at the USA.

Here I will use CARA (Center for Applied Research in the Apostolate)

	1970	2020
Number of		
Priests	59,192	35,513
Sisters	160,931	41,357
Brothers	11,623	3,801
Parishes	18,224	16,703
Parishes without Priests	571	3,544
Official Catholics	47.9m	67.7m
Catholics by survey	54.1m	72.4m
Former Catholics	3.5m	29.5m

Catholic Education

CCD (elementary Sunday School)	4.2m	2.1m
K-8 (parochial)	3.4m	1.2m
Teen CCD (Sunday)	1.3m	550,170
High School (parochial)	1.008m	555,901

Sacraments and Rites

Baptisms	1.089m	545,710
Adult Baptisms	84,534	35,799
Marriage	426,309	131,827

Worldwide

Priests	419,728	545,710
Population	653.6m	1.329b

—It has been stated by multiple sources, although sadly I can't document the sources here, that between the close of the Council '65 and '70 that about fifty thousand priests left the active ministry worldwide. Thus, you can see that the Church has not made up even the loss from '70, and yet the number of Catholics has more than doubled. Also the average age of the priests has risen significantly in recent decades.

Surveys on Faith	**1970**	**2020**
Weekly Mass	54.9%	23.4%
Monthly Mass	71.3%	49.5%
Belief in the Real Presence	63%	30% (2019 Pew Research)

Confession	**2008**
Once a month	2%
Several times a year	12%
Once a year	12%
Less than once a year	30%
Never	45%

—For those that go to mass weekly, 62% go to confession at least once a year. Thus, only 62% of Catholics are doing the absolute minimum required by Church law. I.e.: Mass on Holy Days of Obligation, Confession once a year.

Crisis? What? I'm fine, honestly, I have another leg...
     The above is just a brief overview of the current and recent situation in the Church. It had been promised that the changes implemented would result in a more vibrant Church. The Protestants would come home; atheists and pagans would convert in large numbers; there would be vocations galore; many more

would be married and have children. I can understand, a little, if people fell for this sales pitch in the '60's and even into the '70's, but by the '80's this old hippy talk was a bit... stale. How can anyone look around, being honest, and not say the Church is in a major crisis? Up to this point I haven't even really brought up the reality of the homosexual predators in the clergy or the pedophiles.

Even in the light of these statistics and the massive scandals in the Church, which have resulted in the loss of moral leadership in society, many in the upper hierarchy (bishops) do and say nothing. As some have pointed out, if anyone ran a business with these types of numbers, they would either have to close the doors, or they would have been fired. There was a bishop in the US that refused to ordain anyone, until he was granted permission to ordain woman. The diocese had no new priest for decades. Not only did this joker hold an idea that is clearly heretical, he punished his own flock, and nothing was done. There are many cases of homosexual predators which have not only not been punished, but have too often caused an elevation in clerical rank, thus allowing them to prey on even more victims.

St. John Eudes wrote in *The Priest, His Dignity and Obligations*:

> "The most evident mark of God's anger and the most terrible castigation He can inflict upon the world are manifested when He permits His people to fall into the hands of clerics who are priests more in name than in deed, priests who practice the cruelty of ravening wolves rather than the charity and affection of devoted shepherds. Instead of nourishing those committed to their care, they rend and devour them brutally. Instead of leading their people to God, they drag Christian souls into hell in their train. Instead of being the salt of the earth and the light of the world, they are its innocuous poison and its murky darkness. St. Gregory the Great says that priests and pastors will stand condemned before God as the murderers of any souls lost through neglect or silence....
>
> "When God permits such things, it is a very positive proof that He is thoroughly angry with His people, and is visiting His most dreadful anger upon them. That is why He cries unceasingly to Christians, 'Return, 0 ye revolting children... and I will give you pastors according to my own

heart' (Jer. 3, 14-15). Thus, irregularities in the lives of priests constitute a scourge visited upon the people in consequence of sin."[xxii]

The simple reality is that the Church, indeed the world, is in crisis. The reason is simple and yet hard. We have lost our way. The Lord taught that He is the "Way, the Truth, and the Life", yet even the popes put their trust and hope in modern science and inventions. "The newest thing" has left people always looking for a fix or a quick solution to the troubles of life. It started with new things, but quickly devolved into people looking for an actual fix, i.e.; drugs, sex, rock and roll. These emotional "highs" always lead to a deeper low. Thus the desire for a "higher high".

The answer is simple but not easy. As we find ourselves in the darkness of our times we have to slow down, light a candle as people have for millennia, and search for the answers that led people of the past into the light. New, advanced technology has not changed the condition of fallen man one iota; it has only given him new tools and new ways to destroy himself. I am not here saying that new technology is bad, per se. But all tools have to be used in the proper way, at the proper time, in proportion to the end for which they were made, and may or may not help us. Years ago man invented the chainsaw, helpful, but its usefulness is limited in life.

When I was in the seminary, just out of college, I discovered and learned most of the things in the above chapters. It was not until I was in the seminary that I even knew the church I had grown up in, was kind of invented in the '60's. I was furious; I felt robbed and cheated. I have always been a studier of history and did not know, until then, that all the saints I read about, all the historic music and art inspired to raise the hearts and minds of people, were actually inspired by a different liturgy: a whole other way of living the sacramental and spiritual life, the heart of a Christendom that I had only heard the whispers of, a bygone era that no longer existed. Once I started to study the way the Church actually used to be, it started to make sense. On the one hand the new popular music, terrible art, communist-looking buildings including churches and more, fit naturally with the *Novus Ordo*. On the other hand, the traditional buildings, music, and art fit more naturally with the Traditional Rites.

Now more than fifty years after Vatican II, where are the Catholic artists? Show me a new and beautiful Catholic statue, painting, or piece of music. There are gifted people today, but they are inspired by the *Novus Ordo*, where are the artistic ideas from a more Catholic era? I would argue that the above statistics, the current lack of faith and practice, while not exclusively, are still the result of the new rites that also brought a whole new language and ethos into the Church.

I think this whole reality of a new way of Catholicism, is exactly what Pope Paul VI identified as "the smoke of Satan". I say we get some strong fans, and blow that smoke on out. The fact that the local language is so often used has resulted in the idea of a national type of Catholicism. No longer is the faith universal, no longer Catholic. The rise of national identity and a national faith is destroying the old universality of the faith. One Faith, One Baptism, One Lord of All, using one sacred language to express this important reality.

The principle of the excluded middle, what to do about Vatican II?

Why do I now bring up this principle of logic? It has to do with arguments for or against Vatican II. It is often stated, on the one hand, that Vatican II is a Council which is part of the Ordinary Magisterium, and thus everyone must obey all its teachings. On the other hand it is stated that the Council is not dogmatic, only pastoral, and thus can be ignored. So what about this principle?

In logic, the law of excluded middle (or the principle of excluded middle) states **that for every proposition, either this proposition or its negation is true**. Another Latin designation for this law is *tertium non datur*: "no third [possibility] is given". It is a tautology. In mathematical logic a tautology is a formula or assertion which is true in every possible formulation. For example, "either the ball is green, or the ball is not green" is always true, regardless of the color of the ball. This principle should not be confused with the semantical principle of bivalence, which states that every proposition is either true or false.

Thus with this principle now in hand, is the first statement true? Actually yes and no. Based on the statements of John XIII before the council, that it is pastoral, and Paul VI after the council, that it is pastoral and has no dogmas in it, besides those quoted from previous councils, then it is Ordinary Magisterium. Many have written about the difference between Ordinary and *Extra*ordinary Magisterial statements. For us let's just say, declaring dogma that requires a teaching to be held by all Catholics for all time, is Extraordinary Magisterium. Ordinary are those directives, based on the perennial dogmas, canons, and customs, which are the application of those teachings, laws, and traditions, in a given time and place.

Thus the Bishops together under the Pope have Ordinary powers (like at a council). Bishops in their own diocese have Ordinary powers. However, these powers only bind while they are enforced. For example, there is a diocese some years ago that the bishop forbade his priests from going into bars of any kind. The current bishop has the right to say, go ahead. Ordinary. The same bishop or even the Pope can never say that they don't believe Our Lady was Immaculately Conceived. Extraordinary means a truth taught infallibly by a council and binding all Catholics, of all times, to believe with religious submission of the mind and will.

Therefore Vatican II can't just be ignored, just as someone's bishop can't just be ignored, but, as it is merely pastoral, it only binds for a time on those aspects that do not conflict with previous dogmas, laws, and traditions. Thus using the above principle, both of those statements, blindly follow Vatican II and ignore it outright, are incorrect. I would add that as the documents of Vatican II are in many cases ambiguous and self-contradictory, clarity is desperately needed either way.

Do we have Heaven's response to Vatican II? In the next chapter, we look at the major apparition of Our Lady to occur after the close of the council.

Chapter 11[xxiii]
Our Lady of Akita, Japan, 1973-79, Oct. 6, 2019

In this chapter we will look at the apparition of Our Lady in Akita, Japan. This apparition is the primary one to have taken place after the Second Vatican Council, which we examined in the previous chapter, and therefore we will learn Our Lady's response to this council, the results of it, and the current state of the Church. Then, we will look at how we can amend our lives according to Our Lady's most recent instructions.

Akita Japan was the final place bombed by the USA during WWII. In the afternoon of August 14, 1945, a message from the Emperor Hirohito, recorded, was sent out over the airwaves and said that all imperial forces were to stand down immediately. USAAF 315th Bombardment Wing was eating dinner in the mess hall when the American radios announced the news. They immediately started to celebrate. Some hours later, they were told that the bombing that had already been planned for that evening was to commence as scheduled, and it did. The last bombs dropped in the early hours of the next day, killing over 300 civilians and injuring some 200, the last of the war.

August 15th is the Feast of the Assumption of the Blessed Virgin Mary. Catholic tradition teaches that just as Our Lord arose from the dead on Easter morning, moments after midnight, so, too, Our Lady arose bodily moments after midnight to be assumed into Heaven. What are we to think about this even, at exactly this time, bombs were being dropped on civilians of a country that had already surrendered?

A few pious women known as the Institute of the Handmaids of the Holy Eucharist were leading a quiet, hidden life of prayer in Yuzawadai just outside of Akita, when they welcomed into their novitiate Sister Agnes Katsuko Sasagawa, who was then 42 years old and a convert from Buddhism. When she entered on May 12, 1973, Agnes was totally and incurably deaf, but she was blessed with various mystical favors. Soon this convent would become so well known that their little chapel would attract pilgrims from all around the world.

The first miraculous event at Akita occurred on June 12, 1973, only a month after the entrance of Sr. Agnes. A brilliant light shone forth from the Tabernacle. This happened several times and was often accompanied by something resembling smoke which hung around the altar. During one of these illuminations, Sr. Agnes saw "a multitude of beings similar to Angels who surrounded the altar in adoration before the Host". Bishop Ito was staying at the convent to conduct a week of devotions. Sr. Agnes confided to him the circumstances of this vision, as well as all the events and apparitions that followed. Bishop Ito and the convent's spiritual director, Rev. Teiji Yasuda, were witnesses to many of the events.

Sr. Agnes was also favored with visitations of her guardian angel. Asked to describe the angel, Sr. Agnes replied: "a round face, an expression of sweetness… a person covered with a shining whiteness like snow…." The guardian Angel confided various messages to the sister and often prayed with her, in addition to guiding and advising her.

On the evening of June 28, 1973, Sr. Agnes discovered on the palm of her left hand a cross-shaped wound that was exceedingly painful. On July 5, 1973, a small opening appeared in the center from which blood began to flow. Later, the pain would ease during most of the week except for Thursday nights and all day Friday, when the pain became almost unbearable.

First Message

On July 6, the guardian angel appeared, telling Sr. Agnes: "The wounds of Mary are much deeper and more sorrowful than yours. Let us go to pray together in the chapel." After entering the chapel the angel disappeared. Sr. Agnes then turned to the statue of Mary situated on the right side of the altar.

The statue, which is approximately three feet tall, had been carved from the hard wood of the Judea tree: it is a figure of Our Lady standing before a cross, her arms at her side with the palms of her hands facing forward. Beneath her feet is a globe representing the world.

When Sr. Agnes approached the statue, she said, "I suddenly felt that the wooden statue came to life and was about to speak to me… She was bathed in a brilliant light… and at the same moment a voice of indescribable beauty struck my totally deaf ears." Our Lady told her: "…your deafness will be healed…." She then recited with Sr. Agnes the community prayer that had been composed by Bishop Ito. At the words, "Jesus present in the Eucharist", Mary instructed, "From now on, you will add TRULY." Together with the angel who again appeared, the three voices recited a consecration to the Most Sacred Heart of Jesus, TRULY present in the Holy Eucharist. Before disappearing, Our Lady asked that Sr. Agnes "pray very much for the Pope, bishops and priests...."

The next morning, when the sisters assembled for the recitation of Lauds, they found blood on the right hand of the statue and two lines which crossed, in the middle of which was an opening from which the blood flowed. The wound matched that on the hand of Sr. Agnes, except that, since the statue's hand was smaller, its wound was smaller. It bled on the Fridays of July during the year 1973, as did the wound on the hand of Sr. Agnes.

One of the sisters wrote: "It seemed to be truly cut into flesh. The edge of the cross had the aspect of human flesh and one even saw the grain of the skin like a fingerprint. I said to myself at that moment that the wound was real...."

Of special noteworthiness, the drops of blood ran the length of the statue's hand, which was open and pointing downward, yet the drops never fell from the hand.

The wound on the hand of Sr. Agnes appeared on Thursday, June 28. As predicted by the guardian angel, the wound disappeared on Friday, July 27, without leaving a trace.

Second Message
The second message of Our Lady came on August 3, 1973, a First Friday, when the heavenly voice from the statue warned:

> "My daughter, my novice, do you love the Lord? If you love the Lord, listen to what I have to say to you.
> "It is very important...You will convey it to your superior.
> "Many men in this world afflict the Lord. I desire souls to console Him to soften the anger of the Heavenly Father. I wish, with my Son, for souls who will repair by their suffering and their poverty for the sinners and ingrates.

"In order that the world might know His anger, the Heavenly Father is preparing to inflict a great chastisement on all mankind. With my Son I have intervened so many times to appease the wrath of the Father. I have prevented the coming of calamities by offering Him the sufferings of the Son on the Cross, His Precious Blood, and beloved souls who console Him forming a cohort of victim souls. Prayer, penance, and courageous sacrifices can soften the Father's anger. I desire this also from your community... that it love poverty, that it sanctify itself and pray in reparation for the ingratitude and outrages of so many men.

"Recite the prayer of the Handmaids of the Eucharist with awareness of its meaning; put it into practice; offer in reparation (whatever God may send) for sins. Let each one endeavor, according to capacity and position, to offer herself entirely to the Lord.

"Even in a secular institute prayer is necessary. Already souls who wish to pray are on the way to being gathered together. Without attaching too much attention to the form, be faithful and fervent in prayer to console the Master.

After a silence:

"Is what you think in your heart true? Are you truly decided to become the rejected stone? My novice, you who wish to belong without reserve to the Lord, to become the spouse worthy of the Spouse, make your vows knowing that you must be fastened to the Cross with three nails. These three nails are poverty, chastity, and obedience. Of the three, obedience is the foundation. In total abandon, let yourself be led by your superior. He will know how to understand you and to direct you."[xxiv]

When Sr. Agnes was professed, she pronounced these three vows. Although the wound on the hand of Sr. Agnes disappeared on July 27, the wound on the hand of the statue remained until September 29. At that time the statue emitted a bright light. The wound had remained for three months.

While wounds in the hands of the statue bled, Bishop Ito said that, contrary to some reports, "...the statue did not sweat blood or weep blood at any time."

On the evening office of September 29, 1973, the whole community saw a brilliant light coming from the statue. Almost immediately the entire body of the statue became covered with a moisture resembling perspiration. Sr. Agnes's guardian angel told her, "Mary is even sadder than when she shed blood. Dry the perspiration." The sisters used cotton balls to collect the moisture. Following Our Lady's message, the dazzling light that had surrounded the statue gradually disappeared.

Toward the end of May, 1974, another phenomenon occurred. While the statue's garment and the hair retained the look of natural wood, the face, hands and feet became distinguished by a dark, reddish-brown tint. Eight years later, when the sculptor came to see the statue, he could not hide his surprise that only the visible parts of Our Lady's body had changed color, and that the face itself had changed expression.

Then on January 4, 1975, to the amazement of the community and Fr. Yasuda, the statue of the Virgin began to weep and did so three times that day. Also witnessing these tears, in addition to the sisters, were Bishop Ito and a number of people who had joined the nuns for a New Year's retreat. In the 10 years following, scientific studies excluded any explanation other than the supernatural.

The tears collected on the inside edge of the eyes, flowed down the cheeks, collected at the edge of the garment near the throat, rolled down the folds of the garment and fell upon the globe under Our Lady's feet.

Fr. Yasuda recorded in his book, *The Tears and Message of Mary*, that the statue:

"…had completely dried out during the years since it was made and little cracks had begun to appear. It is already miraculous if water would flow from such material, but it is still more prodigious that a liquid slightly salty, of the nature of true human tears, should have flowed precisely from the eyes."

Eventually, Bishop Ito arranged for Professor Sagisaka, M.D., a non-Christian specialist in forensic medicine, to make a rigorous scientific examination of the three fluids, although the Bishop did not reveal their source. The results were: "The matter adhering on the gauze is human blood. The sweat and the tears absorbed in the two pieces of cotton are of human origin." The blood was found to belong to group B and the sweat and tears to group AB. Sr. Agnes belongs to group B.

Bishop Ito was advised by the Apostolic Nuncio to seek the assistance of the Archbishop of Tokyo in creating a commission of canonical inquiry. Unfortunately, the Inquisitor (government investigator) who was not Catholic, was named president of this group. Without any of the members visiting the convent to conduct a personal inquiry, the commission rendered an unfavorable verdict.

Unwilling to accept a negative verdict to the events he himself had witnessed, Bishop Ito asked the advice in Rome of the Congregation for the Doctrine of the Faith, as well as the Congregation for the Propagation of the Faith. He was then advised to form another commission to study the events from the beginning. This commission rendered a favorable verdict regarding the supernatural aspects of the events.

The tears of December 8, 1979 were filmed by a television crew at 11 o'clock in the evening, the Feast of the Immaculate Conception, and was shown on television to 12 million people throughout Japan. It is now shown by the nuns at the convent and was shown during news broadcasts throughout the world.

The sculptor of the statue, Saburo Wakasa, a non-Catholic and a citizen of Akita, was asked his reaction to the occurrences relating to the statue. He answered:

"The statue of Mary was my first work connected with Christianity. Of my various statues, it is only with the statue of Mary at Yuzawadai that mysterious events occurred... I sculptured the whole statue of Mary, globe, and the Cross from the same piece of wood, so there are no joints. The wood from which I carved the statue of Mary was very dry and rather hard...." When questioned as to whether he regards as a "miracle" the reported shedding of tears from the statue of Mary, he replied, "It is a mystery."

Another examination of the fluids was conducted by Dr. Sagisaka of the Department of Forensic Medicine, School of Medicine, University of Akita. The results were given on November 30, 1981, and revealed that: "The object examined has adhering to it human liquids which belong to the blood group O." Since the first analysis revealed that the blood belonged to group B and the sweat and tears to group AB, it has been established that the fluids belong to three different blood groups.

It is a medical fact that the blood, tears, and sweat of an individual all belong to the same blood group. One fluid cannot differ in type from the other fluids of the same body. Since Sr. Agnes belonged to group B she could not have "ejected and transferred" blood or fluids belonging to group AB or O. The theory of the Inquisitor that Sr. Agnes exercised her ectoplasmic power (essentially a form of witchcraft) was thereby refuted.

On the Feast of Our Lady of Sorrows (September 15), the statue cried for the last time. Two weeks later, Sr. Agnes's guardian angel presented a large Bible surrounded with a brilliant light. The open Bible revealed the reference, Genesis 3:15. The angel explained that the passage had a relationship with the tears of Mary and then continued "... sin came into the world by a woman and it is also by a woman that salvation came to the world...."

The lachrymations (weepings) number 101 occurences, and they took place at irregular intervals from January 4, 1975 until September 15, 1981. The first "1" is Eve, the second, Our Lady, and the "0" represents the eternal Holy Trinity.

According to the records kept by the sisters, the number of persons witnessing the tears went unrecorded on five occasions. However, all the other times they were witnessed by no fewer than ten persons, and other lachrymations were witnessed by various numbers of people, sometimes as many as 46, 55 and, for the last lachrymation, 65 people. Some of the witnesses were non-Christians and some were prominent Buddhists, including the mayor of the city.

Third Message

On October 13, 1973, the anniversary of the Miracle of the Sun at Fatima, Sr. Agnes heard the beautiful voice speaking from the statue once more:

> She continued, "As I told you, if people do not repent and better themselves, the Father will inflict a terrible punishment on all humanity. It will be a punishment greater than the Flood, such as one will never have seen before. Fire will fall from the sky and will wipe out a great part of humanity, the good as well as the bad, sparing neither priests nor faithful. The survivors will find

themselves so desolate that they will envy the dead. The only arms which will remain for you will be the Rosary and the Sign left by my Son. Each day recite the prayers of the Rosary. With the Rosary pray for the Pope, the bishops, and the priests."

"The work of the devil will infiltrate even into the Church in such a way that one will see cardinals opposing cardinals, bishops against other bishops. The priests who venerate me will be scorned and opposed by their confreres; churches and altars will be sacked. The Church will be full of those who accept compromises, and the devil will press many priests and consecrated souls to leave the service of the Lord. The demon would be especially implacable against souls consecrated to God. The thought of the loss of so many souls is the cause of my sadness. If sins increase in number and gravity, there will be no longer any pardon for them."

The statue wept for the last time on September 15, Feast of Our Lady of Sorrows.

Sr. Agnes was totally and incurably deaf when she entered the community, having lost her hearing on March 16, 1973. She was able to speak, and understood spoken messages by lip reading. As predicted by her guardian angel, she temporarily regained her hearing on October 13, 1974. Deafness returned on March 7, 1975. Her hearing was permanently restored on May 30, 1982, as predicted by Our Lady during the first message of July 6, 1973. Both healings occurred instantaneously during Benediction of the Blessed Sacrament. Sr. Agnes is today in sound health, except for the rheumatism that has affected her hands.

A canonical law regarding the judgment of a Marian apparition was issued in 1978. According to a Vatican official: "...the authority to hand down a conclusion regarding the authenticity of any Marian apparition is given canonically to the ordinary (the bishop) of the local diocese where the apparition took place...."

In his pastoral letter dated April 22, 1984, Bishop John Ito, the Ordinary of the Diocese of Niigata, wrote that having been given directives in this regard, "I authorize throughout the entire diocese of which I am charged, the veneration of the Holy Mother of Akita." The Bishop noted that the events are only a matter of private revelation and are not points of doctrine. The Bishop also mentioned in his pastoral letter that he had known Sr. Agnes Sasagawa for 10 years. "She is a woman sound in spirit, frank and without problems; she has always impressed me as a balanced person. Consequently the messages she says that she has received did not appear to me to be in any way the result of imagination or hallucination."

Four years later, on June 20, 1988, during Bishop Ito's visit to Rome, the Sacred Congregation for the Doctrine of the Faith approved the contents of the pastoral letter. Bishop Ito's official recognitions of the occurrences and the Madonna's messages were reported in the October, 1988 issue of the magazine *30 Days*. In the August 1990 issue, Cardinal Ratzinger is quoted as saying that "there are no objections to the conclusion of the pastoral letter". Cardinal Ratzinger has invited the Bishop to continue to inform him about the pilgrimages and conversions. [xxv]

Then on Oct. 6, 2019, Sr. Agnes received this message, "Cover in ashes, and please pray the Penitential Rosary every day." This day was the opening of the Amazon Synod. On October 4, Pope Francis attended an act of idolatrous worship of the pagan goddess, Pachamama. He allowed this worship to take place in the Vatican Gardens, thus desecrating the vicinity of the graves of the martyrs and of the church of the Apostle Peter. He participated in this act of idolatrous worship by blessing a wooden image of Pachamama. On October 7, the idol of Pachamama was placed in front of the main altar at St. Peter's and then carried in procession to the Synod Hall. Pope Francis said prayers in a ceremony involving this image and then joined in this procession. When wooden images of this pagan deity were removed from the church of Santa Maria in Traspontina, where they had been sacrilegiously placed, and thrown into the Tiber by Catholics outraged by this profanation of the church, Pope Francis, on October 25, apologized for their removal and another wooden image of Pachamama was returned to the church. Thus, a new profanation was initiated. On October 27, in the closing Mass for the synod, he accepted a bowl used in the idolatrous worship of Pachamama and placed it on the altar. 1260 days later will be April 9, 2023, Easter Sunday, (from the prophet Daniel, time, times and half a time, 1260 days, with the

140

Jewish 360 day year, after the enthronement of the "abomination of desolation").

Commentary

The things that strike me the most about these events are the weeping of Our Lady. Some would incorrectly conclude that those blessed souls in Heaven are not affected by our actions down here on Earth. Clearly the sadness of Our Lady, the real effects of our sins are not only a burden, but one we should take seriously. Also Sister Agnes was a deaf convert. In giving this message to her, it's as if Our Lady is showing that she can and will give her message to the deaf, even new converts.

The First Message July 6, 1973

"Pray very much for the Pope, Bishops, and Priests. Since your Baptism you have always prayed faithfully for them. Continue to pray very much...very much. Tell your superior all that passed today and obey him in everything that he will tell you. He has asked that you pray with fervor."

Here we see a similar message as the first at Fatima, pray very much. Also the prayer of her community is a witness to the reality of the Real Presence of the Body, Blood, Soul, and Divinity of Christ in the Eucharist, Truly Present.

The Second Message, August 3, 1973

"Many men in this world afflict the Lord. I desire souls to console Him to soften the anger of the Heavenly Father. I wish, with my Son, for souls who will repair by their suffering and their poverty for the sinners and ingrates...."

Here again this message follows the pattern of Fatima, due to the sins and offenses that afflict the Lord, we must console and soften the anger of God. If we do not, Our Lady warns of a chastisement that will be sent. Our Lady speaks of victim souls, people that offer their sufferings to mediate the punishments which are due. Here I think of St. Padre Pio, who asked to suffer for the salvation of souls. He was given the stigmata, the wounds of

Christ. They actually bled until his death. Moments after he died, the wounds were completely gone.

The Third Message, October 13, 1973

Due to the offenses of our sins, Divine Justice demands some kind of retribution; call it a balancing of debts. However, as God is both perfectly just and merciful, and in order to save souls, He has warned through Our Lady that He will chastise the World. Not only for the sake of justice, but also mercy.

> "It will be a punishment greater than the Flood, such as one will never have seen before. Fire will fall from the sky and will wipe out a great part of humanity, the good as well as the bad, sparing neither priests nor faithful. The survivors will find themselves so desolate that they will envy the dead. The only arms which will remain for you will be the Rosary and the Sign left by my Son. Each day recite the prayers of the Rosary. With the Rosary pray for the Pope, the bishops and the priests."

Here we see both the warning and the solution. Repent, pray the Rosary, entrust everything and everyone you love, to Our Lady. Also a sign, or indication, that the chastisement is coming closer is the infiltration of even the highest ranks of the Church. "Cardinal will fight Cardinal, Bishop will fight Bishop." The interesting thing here is that of course bishops and cardinals have fought each other from the beginning, that is not new. What is new now is that these fights have been brought into the open. In these recent years and weeks we see ever increasing fights in the upper Hierarchy, just as Our Lady promised. The threat of an event that is '"greater than the Flood" and that it will result in the "greater part of humanity being wiped out" is rather ominous.

On this point it has been noted that the billions of poor babies that have been murdered in their own mothers' wombs cry out for vengeance. Just as the blood of Abel cried out and was given justice, so now the blood of these innocents cry out. In strict justice, billions of babies that the Lord sent and gave to world were summarily murdered, so now billions of people that either perpetrated these crimes, simply stood by, or tried to stop it but were unsuccessful, will pay the price of blood with their own blood. It is a modern error which that only sees the mercy of God. His mercy is only given, "in the light of His justice". Thus this warning reveals the coming of His justice. While the killing of innocent life is terrible, this is by no means the only crime against humanity that these days has been, not only legalized, but very often promoted.

Finally we are told that the priests who have devotion to Our Lady will be persecuted; how many priests have been sidelined for preaching the Gospel? How many Churches have been sacked, altars desecrated? How many people and clergy, fill the churches that have compromised the true faith as Our Lady warns us? For example, do we believe the Lord is "the Way, the Truth, and the Light, and nobody comes to the Father except through Him"? This means what the Church has always taught, *extra Ecclesiam non salla,* outside the Church there is no salvation.

On the contrary, most of the "Catholics" I have met over the years don't think there is any danger for those outside the Church to go to Hell, "so long as they believe". Believe what exactly? That pizza is better with beer perhaps? We know that *only* 30% of weekly Mass-goers believe in the Real Presence. I think the Church is indeed full of those who have compromised. The worst thing about what is in this chapter is that eternal, beautiful souls are at risk, and eternity is forever.

Chapter 12
Finally,
What Do We Do?

In this final chapter I want to point out some of the major points which we have looked at in the previous chapter with some observations that I think are relevant to our time. In the final portion, I will make some recommendations based on those observations.

<u>Observations and Comments</u>
One point that I hope is now clear is this: ideas have consequences. It seems like a rather simple, obvious, and straightforward proposition. However, many people, even if they agree in principle with this, practically disregard it in their lives. How can this be? Let's take a quick recap of what I have attempted to bring out thus far. Starting with the current situation— Christendom destroyed, Modernism reigning supreme. This was simply to point out that the society built up on the bedrock of Christian principles has been replaced, could we say eclipsed, by Modernism. How did this happen? It took some time, but the separation of faith and reason leads to separation of Church and State. Let us think of society as a boat; the teachings and morals handed down the centuries are the rudder. Thus with the silencing of the Church, society becomes like a ship without a rudder.
Further, the silencing of the Church leads to Materialism and Egoism. This seemingly subtle but important shift changed the general outlook of people from a God-centered and -driven life, to a man-, or better yet, *me*-centered life. Ask yourself, do you live to work, or do you work to live? And what is life all about? Classically, the Christian would answer "to know and serve God in this life, so as to reign with Him in the next". What is your answer, or what do you observe drives society today? Man-centered thinking is realized in Romanticism and lack of logic because the higher faculties of man, thinking and reason, have been subjected to the lower faculties of man, feeling and intuition. This flip-flop of the natural order leads to a failure of clear, objective thinking and results in the dictatorship of Relativism. This dictatorship allows for no dissenters. The one rule is, everyone makes up their own

rules, so long as your little kingdom impedes no other kingdom. Or to put it in modern parlance, "live and let live". But what is wrong with that you might ask? The fundamental problem is that we are made for God, the path to God is laid out by Him, and thus we are compelled to conform to His Will in order to walk that path. Of course, if one does not have supernatural faith, and this life is all there is, then yes, just be kind and let others do whatever they want. This is what most people think these days. This is also wrong and antithetical to Christianity. The Christian is called to love God above all else, including the self, and to show this love in love of neighbor. Now what kind of neighbor lets those around them do and commit self-harm?

Let's take a very brief overview of how we got here. In this next section I will go over the major ideas and their consequences. In the following section I will go over the messages from Heaven, namely some of the most important notes from Our Lady. As we go through, let me point out a couple of things. First, in terms of history, it is true in that we are moving inexorably toward the end of time. Every day we are closer to that moment than the day the before. However, history is also a series of repeated events. In the Book of Ecclesiastes 1:9, we are told "there is nothing new under the sun". This is referring to exactly my point. The basic pattern of fallen man repeats itself over and over again. Obviously there are new things, certainly new people, new technologies, but fallen man has an amazing ability to repeat the same mistakes which those before have made.

Second, the messages of God and the ways that He tries to call to correction fallen man, also repeats itself. Well, not exactly repeats because God has always been, will always be, and never changes. The basic pattern is the same, yet the means change. For example there was the time of Noah, a call to repentance resulting in the Flood; Moses's gathering of the people, who were given their own land for the sake of proper worship, resulting in exile and final loss of land and temple; and now the time of Christ which changes everything, giving the world to His Church to save souls, and yet over the centuries we see times of great sanctity and times of chastisement (North Africa and the Middle East were lost because of heresy and a lack of obedience to proper authority, the Pope).

So in this sense the pattern is this: God gives to man revelation about Himself and thus a clearer understanding of Him; you cannot love Whom you do not know. Men are initially happy and faithful, but, to varying speeds and degrees, they forget, lose heart, and turn away. The Lord calls to conversion, and sometimes they convert and sometimes not, and when they don't, chastisement ensues. For example, at the end of the 14th century, it was noted that Christendom was the worst that it had ever been, and many thought the end of the world was at hand. To this century, the Lord sent St. Vincent Ferrer (1350-1419) who for twenty years preached all over Europe to Christians that if they did not repent, the Last Judgment was imminent. There was a massive conversion, or really reversion, to Catholic life, and the punishment was averted. As we have seen at other times, the requests of the Lord have been ignored. Remember the French kings' indifference leading to the Reign of Terror, also known as the French Revolution. Here now, we will look at how the fallen have infected the minds of man and spread errors, leading to our time, the worst in human history.

From the Greeks to Modern time

The ancient Greeks left us many valuable lessons. In general, we can say that the various areas of human study were brought together into a kind of system. This we call a school. Most famous is the "school at Athens". The method that was developed was exactly what we all think of as a school, a systematic study of things. Indeed, Athens remains famous precisely because of this system and method, and added to this was the idea that no subjects were off limits and that someone became proficient when they could teach and defend their propositions on their feet in public, rhetoric. However, there were those that did not care about "finding the truth"; they only wanted to sway the hearts and minds of the people, the sophists. Here we see the first real split in academic studies and the rise of the professional "public speaker". Some of these men used their ability for political ends, others for financial ends, still others for the joy of it. We still have all these types today, politicians, advertisers, and entertainers. Thus, a question is realized, what is the point of knowledge, understanding, and speaking?

One of the other things that the Greeks left us besides this fundamental question of education is another question: how is a person to deal with a systematic study of those things that are beyond the physical realm? This question of "metaphysics", the study of those first principles that are "beyond physical". It is exactly this study that begins to answer the above questions, what is the point of education, why are we here, what is next? In answer to these questions, two schools arise. Some wanted to say only the physical is knowable and thus truly real, while others say absolutely not: the "metaphysical" in fact is more real than the physical. As you might guess, the metaphysical carried the day, with Plato and Aristotle.

However, the fight was far from over. The physical-only argument, as I tried to show in chapters 4, 6, and 7, has made a major comeback in the form of the materialists. Think of this; when asked which hypothesis is more readily provable, what do you think? First: the idea of the Big Bang: everything in the universe starting all compacted, and then a "big bang" making a massive expansion and thus the "start" of the universe as we know it. Second: the all-knowing, all-powerful God made everything from nothing. Would you be surprised to find out that the theory of the big bang was already practically disproven in the time of the Greeks, and that today high-end astrophysicists both can prove it doesn't work and also that if it were to work, it still requires "the finger of God" to start it. God creating everything out of nothing is still the only logical beginning of an explanation we have for "how we got here". So how did you do? Did you find the thesis of the bang more probable? I use this example to show how much these ideas have become a part of everyone's thinking; we are all at least a little modernist and materialist.

Finally, the Greeks left us with an attempt to separate faith from reason. This is just a necessary result of arguing that the physical world is the only thing that is real. Again, we see historically that metaphysics won out. The Catholics not only have no problem with a unity of faith and reason, but it is actually required for all Catholics to hold to the "Unity of Truth" which is to say that there is only One Source of Truth, God, and all truth is in harmony. Therefore there can be no contests or disagreement between the lower sciences and the higher, between math, chemistry, biology, etc., and soteriology, epistemology, Sacred Scripture, Sacred Tradition, etc. What I have tried to show is that, since the 15th century, an effort has been made to separate faith and reason. More to the point, an effort to subjugate faith to human reason, the idea that everything that faith proposes must be conformable and confirmable by human means, that a degree in medicine makes one able to reform society, without any actual evidence.

On the smallest of pretext, the world was made into a prison for the better part of two years. It is amazing the level of worship that is given to people with an MD. I'll admit that, possibly, for the first few weeks or so, being overly cautious with a strain of the flu that was not fully known could be prudent. But as the weeks went on, and the evidence built up that this one, while possibly more contagious, was actually less deadly than the common flu, it made no difference to people.

We can see here that emotion has been raised above intellect, feelings over logic. Also the lower sciences have been placed above the higher sciences, reason over faith. It's true that all Catholics have the obligation to do normal reasonable things to take care of their bodies, but this overreaction which so many people just unthinkingly went along with, it is staggering. In these last months we can clearly see the results of the lack of clear thinking as a normal human ability. Reason has been pushed down so far in the lives of so many that they don't even realize how unreasonable turning the world into a prison actually is. Let me be frank, the phrase "lockdown" before last year, was used almost exclusively to describe a reaction to unrest in a prison. This whole charade reveals that the "leaders" not only have no confidence that normal people can make informed decisions about themselves and not put others at undue risk, but that they have the right to dictate to everyone what is allowed and not. All the while, many of these leaders did not follow their own rules and had different rules for different groups. If one wanted to buy liquor or weed, it was fine, but the same person could not go to church and receive the Most Blessed Sacrament on the tongue while kneeling. I would love to hear a reasonable explanation for that.

The other result of separating faith and reason, with the concomitant effect of raising reason above faith and then placing emotion above reason, is that people now both judge and decide what is "true" based on how they feel. In a Catholic society, God is at the top and is the most important. Christ the King rules the day, and everyone must conform their mind and will to the Mind and Will of God. Thus throughout the days, weeks, months, and years everyone should, even slowly, be able to think and thus act more like God. In contrast, maybe a diabolical contrast, people today have replaced God with themselves. No longer do people conform to the objective truth, rather now, the individual "truth" reigns supreme, the dictatorship of Relativism. What had started out in the Book of Genesis as an invitation to "become like God" in reality results in an attempt to replace God with man, to become your own god. The "I" is now the judge and arbiter of what is true and good. For instance, how many males today argue against their own gender and "decide" to "become a woman". You see this is an attempt to "be like God", to replace Him with man. No one can replace God, men only reject their proper end and their only true good, the source of true and endless joy and peace, God.

Just as in the modern world, man has replaced God with himself on the personal level, so too man has replaced God with himself on the societal level. As I said above, in a Catholic society, Christ is the true King, the earthly rulers are given authority by Him, and are going to have to answer to Him for everything they do and don't do for His people that He placed under them. Thus the Church has always taught, authority comes from above (cf John 19:1). This means that authority goes from God, the supreme authority, to His Vicar on Earth, then to the bishops, priests, deacons, kings, princes, counts, and so on. In Christendom, it was rare that a pope even tried to remove those in lesser authority; even when a pope wrote that the Emperor was subject to him, it caused some trouble for the pope.

Today, however, the Kingship of Christ is totally ignored. Even while the US was never a Catholic nation, there were some references to our nation as "being under God" in the past. Now, with murder of babies, males becoming female, etc., obviously there is not even reference to the Divine Will. This is all justified by the ridiculously false notion that power comes "from the people". Logically, of course, this makes no sense, given how power is used. If power came from the people, how exactly was slavery justified, or how are babies murdered today? Or are we to believe that the power to govern, handed over by the people, is a transitory truth? In other words, babies somehow earn this power when they breathe? Or slaves earn this power when... actually I have no idea how one could complete that sentence as the premise is so ridiculous.

No, the fact that power and authority clearly doesn't, and never could, come from the people is shown in a cursory study of history. There were slaves; the fact of slavery shows by itself that authority comes from above. Another way to put it is this: if authority came from the men themselves, who in their right mind, having the authority, would choose to be a slave? No, slavery shows that authority comes above and that fallen man can misuse the authority given. History is replete with bad rulers that are punished for not properly using their authority. Again, what baby would choose to be murdered?

In the Apparitions of Our Lady in Quito, Ecuador,1594-1634, covered in Chapter 3, we were warned that the Masonic sects would rule nearly every aspect of life in our times. There have been many books written that describe how they infiltrated the Church and society, governments, commerce, etc. Let's quickly look at the errors of "freemasonry": rejection of Christ and His Church, rejection of God-made man, exaltation of man-made god, rejection of the supernatural, exaltation of the natural, and thus a religion of Naturalism, being brothers in a "natural" way. They have lauded the efforts of some recent church men for "Ecumenism". In this they see the Masonic idea of "one religion" taking shape. Their version is not the Catholic reality that there is One God, and thus One True Religion, Catholicism. No, they want a "religion" that allows and encompasses all religions at the same time. It seems like the warnings of Our Lady of Good Success of the Purification turned out to be true. Make no mistake though; there is only One Way to Heaven, Christ, in and through His body, the Church.

It is said that Abraham Lincoln, quoting Catholic moral teaching, said, "You never have the freedom to choose to do what is wrong." Here is following the idea of a distinction between freedom and liberty. Liberty simply means the ability to do something. Freedom is the ability to choose the good with the result that you are then freer to choose the good again. It's a simple lesson about virtue and vice. Often today, these words are used interchangeably with obfuscation resulting. But remember, liberty was the idea of the French Revolution, the ability to do what you want. Freedom, with its reference to good, implies a higher order in reality. It already points upwards. The point here is that under the

150

appearance of progress and "things getting better", in reality, people are losing, indeed many never had, the ability to think, reason, and choose the good and avoid evil. Those that should be clear in pointing out what is evil and what is good, too often say the opposite and call an evil good and a good evil. Let's look at how these ideas have affected the Church.

All these errors have infected the Church

It has been said that Pope Paul VI meant that the clergy were becoming the problem when he said, "the smoke of Satan has entered the Church." Here I will take this for granted that *some* of the clergy were the problem. Let us then look at how they could be a problem, and how it could have happened. First, the question of how the clergy could be a problem in the Church:

I could just say look at the news for the last twenty or so years, but in reality you could look at the news for the last sixty or so years and find many stories of clergy not acting like clergy. Of course, there are all those incidents of sexual abuse, both of minors and of young adults and even of adults, male and female. There are huge numbers of priests, often within the first few years after ordination, that have left the ministry, bishops that have had to resign, or "retire" because of one scandal or another. There is, or was, a bishop that refused to ordain men until he could ordain women. What nonsense! How about we put a pause on children being born until men can become mothers, too? When you add to this little sad tale the enormous amount of time and money in Church-run education, and most that go through these programs know little of what the Church actually teaches and believe even less, it is quite sad. It becomes very clear that the clergy, some of them, have become a problem in the Church. To renew the Church, renew the Priesthood of Christ. Maybe a new St. Charles Borromeo will come along to reform the clergy. (More on that in a bit.)

The question then remains: how did this happen? The answer will give us some insight in what should be done about it. My hope is that at this point in this little book you might have some ideas, but let's lay them out and see if my train of thought is close to yours. In brief, we can say that the basic ideas as they have already been laid out in this chapter most certainly have infected the thinking of the clergy. That is, the general tendency to think from the personal or subjective point of view, to value your own experience as a primary means of understanding, and thereby to judge reality. This results in placing emotions above intellect.

When this happens to an individual their ability to think and reason is greatly diminished. When they are confronted by two opposing ideas and told the naturally bad idea is good and the good idea is bad this creates what is called "cognitive dissonance". What this means is that our minds are created to see reality as it actually is and learn from others and our own experiences how to choose the good and avoid evil. Fire is good to cook hotdogs but bad for my hand. What happens when a person or people are told over and over again that it's good, even great to put your hand in a fire? Eventually they start to believe it. Ergo, it's good to kill babies so that they are not a burden on the young women. This of course ignores the horrible trauma it causes to the mother and all those involved; no one can kill a child and remain unaffected by it.

So we have people that sometimes think that good is bad and bad is good. This is a terrible situation for any group, but we are told that it is in fact a punishment from God when He allows it within the ranks of the clergy. We have been told by the prophet Jeremiah, and repeated by St. John Eudes, that the worst chastisement the Lord can send on his people is to send them "wolves in sheep's clothing". Therefore when we see, not just a few, but a huge number of wolves, then we realize that the worst punishment the Lord gives his people, He has been giving us for many decades. It is said that a priest brings a bunch of people with him either to glory or to damnation. Sr. Lucy of Fatima, said that the fallen target priests in particular because it is the fastest way to get the most souls condemned. But still the question remains, how did this all happen *inside* the Church?

There are good books that show how the Masonic sects, including the communists, have infiltrated the Church. Also, they show how these infiltrators have found "compromised" seminarians and clergy and manipulated them to their ends. "Compromised" here means everything from having personal sins, for example of a sexual nature, to men being selfish in their desire for prestige, power, or money. Or most often, it means a mix of all possibilities to varying degrees. When you add to this more organized approach, some men who are struggling or confused about their sexuality, and with those who, let's just say are

modernists, we can sum up the list up as follows: intentional
infiltrators, compromised, confused and weak, modernists, and just
run-of-the-mill fallen men. This last group of well-meaning
Catholic men will always be a part of the seminary system. The
first four in our list should never be allowed near a seminary. To
this list and the philosophical issues already talked about, we can
add one more issue that has led to our current crisis.

If you remember back in the second chapter of this book, we
went over some of the historic notes of the Council of Trent and
the aftermath. One of the things that followed Trent was a new
form of obedience. Instead of obedience as the submission of the
mind and will to a lawful rule, request, order, law, etc., it was now
the submission of the will to a superior. The mind, the faculty of
understanding, was omitted; also, the reason and reasonableness
was not taken into account. This novel approach only asked, no,
demanded compliance. It has been said that this entered into the
Society of Jesus about the time of the death of its founder, St.
Ignatius of Loyola. From here, it spread to most of the Orders that
taught in seminaries. Thus, this novel obedience, a blind following,
which is not Christian obedience at all, resulted in a new clerical
culture. This new culture was in large part, though not everywhere,
marked by "the superior and the subject". It had been noted that the
Dominicans fought this novel idea, as well as the Benedictines and
others. But the Jesuits, Salesians, and others, which teach largely in
seminaries, adopted this line of thinking and formation.

This caused the unwritten traditions, the spirit of the
priesthood, to be slowly lost, not in total but in large parts. By the
mid-nineteenth century there developed a movement, the Liturgical
Movement, that had as its principal aim to teach priests about the
liturgy so that they could actually know what they were doing and
thus more fully participate in it. Only in the early twentieth century
did this movement start to look at laity, and this led to the rise of
hand missals for the laity and even their kids. So why or how could
a group like this start?

I would say that as the focus became about "blind obedience"
in the priesthood, the rich spiritual heritage that was normally
handed down by word of mouth and example, fell away. Thus, less
than three hundred years after Trent, many of the priests no longer
knew why they were doing things in the Holy Sacrifice of the
Mass. Of course they knew Latin and the rubrics, and from the
outside it all looked the same, but the spirit of priests, based on a

profound understanding of what every little detail meant and how every part pointed to Christ and salvation, was gone. Only with priests in this state could a new mass, with only seventeen percent of the prayers staying unchanged, the *Novus Ordo* of Paul VI, be introduced while priests and bishops stood by and obediently took it. On the one hand, the atmosphere of blind obedience ran supreme, and on the other hand the priests didn't realize what was being changed and thus what was being taken from them and the Church in general.

This general disposition among the clergy is still present. How many churches have been closed these past months? How many people have not received the sacraments of the dying? How many children have not been baptized in a timely manner? These things were prophesied to us by Our Lady in Ecuador more than 400 years ago. Yet, more was told to us, including the warnings from Japan almost fifty years ago, about "fire from the sky". Yet the worst of the chastisement is clearly already here. The wolves that must be removed, the faith that must restored. Let us pray that the prelate which Our Lady of Good Success of the Purification talked about is quickly sent.

Penance, Penance, Penance!!!

Live a sacramental life, stay in His good graces, and do penance

For us the most important thing is to live a sacramental life. This means to go to Mass as often as possible, with confession at minimum once a month, but every two weeks would be better. As a general rule, the saints down the centuries went once a week, although some at times would go daily. Mass and confession are the baseline of the spiritual life, but without at least a third of the rosary every day one will easily be knocked down. I say a third because five decades, one set of the three mysteries, is a basic minimum. Far better would be to say a whole rosary every day. That's only around 45 minutes. Plus, it is a penance that is very pleasing to God, by meditating on the mysteries of our salvation with Our Lady. Also, physical penances are needed. Wake up at midnight to pray a *Pater Noster* with your arms outstretched. Give up a few meals a week, skip lunch, or have meat at dinner only a few times a week, don't eat meat on Fridays in honor of the Passion, etc.

Is that a new St. Charles Borromeo coming to renew the priesthood?

There is a prelate that is mentioned at some length by Our Lady in Ecuador, who is to renew the spirit of the priesthood, but She says that his coming will be delayed due to the laxity of the priests of that time. I think this is our time. Please pray for this man and that the Lord will send him quickly to be the Divine agent of renewal that is very, very needed today. Also, we need to pray for the spirit of the priesthood; the general atmosphere that many priests are heroically working under these days is not easy, and good holy priests, while always needed, are in dire need these days. Remember we get what we ask for, the Lord gives us what is good for us and for which we ask Him. Are we asking for holy bishops and priests?

Can somebody please hold these bishops accountable?

Thus far I have only written about the accounts of apparitions of Our Lady. However, there are numerous prophesies about our time, mentioning the end or second half of the twentieth century, the turn of the millennia, etc. If you are interested, they can be found, but I recommend only looking at approved things. For example, contained here are all the main apparitions of Our Lady. I know of more and have read them, but they don't add much in the larger picture, and they repeat and agree with the ones contained herein. There are some that are clearly not supernatural. That does not mean the Lord, even in these places, cannot or does not give grace and call people to conversion. But we should be very careful and wait for guidance from proper authorities in the Church before we give our assent to these events. Remember that we have been warned that the fallen angels will try to pass themselves off as angels of light.

I will add one note about the future that is in the visions of many canonized saints. Many of them prophesy about a holy pope that will come, fix, and renew the Church such that the Church will be more glorious than ever before. This gives me great comfort as I watch the horror of our times. Only a pope can discipline Bishops and bring justice where it is needed in the Church. I am reminded that "where sin abounds, grace abounds all the more". We are living in the most sinful times in human history; as bad as that is, it also means the Lord is giving incredible graces and opportunities to become saints. We need saints more than ever; why not you?

So What?

After all this, the ideas, history, and so forth, one might ask the question, so what? So what if all these things happened and the Queen of Heaven has warned us? I seem to remember that Pope John Paul II said in the early '80's that the material chastisement "can no longer be avoided, all we can do is mitigate" how bad it is. Let's take a step back from the details of everyday life and look at the things covered in this little book. Besides the errors of bad philosophy spreading into society to the point that now few are free to think without their emotions clouding their minds, what is the Lord, Master, and King of everything, trying to show us? He is our loving Father, and thus in every punishment, the reason for the punishment, there is a lesson. In part it is that same lesson that has been repeated down the centuries. Too often people want to rule and govern themselves freely, ignoring God.

Here are a few examples: After the chosen people were given land and shown the proper way to offer worship and sacrifice to God, all due to His interventions and winning many battles for them, they wanted their own king. The Lord was to be their only king, but He relented, gave them a king, and shortly thereafter, they turned away from the one God, worshipped demons, Baal, and the like, killing the prophets sent to call them to conversion, and finally losing the whole thing and ending up hauled away to a foreign, pagan land, Babylon.

Years after the Resurrection, the Lord had conquered the greatest empire in history, Rome, taken over its capital, language, and nearly all its lands, and gave all these to the Christians. In response for this largess, the Christians fought *each other* for small pieces of land and "honor". In the meantime, the Lord allowed the "prince of this world" to start a new religion, very militant, and in a very short space of time, all of North Africa, the Middle East, the Holy Land, up to and including present-day Turkey, and most of the Iberian Peninsula, were all lost.

We could go on with these examples, especially when you add in the various plagues, famines, and the like that the Lord has

156

visited on His people in order to call them to conversion. Some might think at this point that this just proves that the Lord is unfair or unjust or some such thing. I would respond with a question: have you ever tried to raise a child or a dog, or train a horse? If so, you will immediately know that sometimes the loving thing to do is discipline them for their own good. So now try to imagine you have made the entire universe including, of course, humans, and you want to save them. You have sent the Second Person of the Trinity to die for them, yet many ignore Him and you have established One Church that is also often ignored, sadly even by those that are technically members. What do you do? With a child you might send them to their room, etc., but how about a world of people? How about if you send the Queen of Heaven, the Mother of All, and what if She shows a miracle more amazing than any for at least a few millennia? Certainly the world will listen to Her, right? Sadly, She, too, has been largely ignored.

The reality is that the spiritual chastisement has been in full force from the 1960's, and it was started at least thirty years before that. All we are waiting for is the next physical chastisement. "Next" because we have already had two world wars, nearly non-stop wars for over one hundred years, hurricanes, earthquakes, and much more. This is a long answer to, "So what?". I think the lesson is the same as many millennia ago: we either follow and submit to the reign of Christ our King, or we get the reign of the fallen, the prince of this world. What we see today is the result of the latter, and I am confident that every day under this regime is worse than the day before. Sure, from time to time, we might slow it down, we might even win a local victory, but we are all the worse for it. The last one hundred years is like the last three years of the so called "Third Reich". It was supposed to rule for a thousand years, yet in the end it was all rubble and ruin.

Do not put your confidence in horses or men, despite their power, they cannot save you. Trust rather in God, and Him alone.

Viva Christo Rey!!!

Fallible Popes

Pope Liberius 352-366: While in exile signed semi-Arian synod *Un Surmium*, composed in 351, which contradicted Nicaea of 357. Semi-Arians wanted a compromise; Nicea said homousious (same substance), not homeousious (similar substance). One letter was thus changed. Liberius excommunicated St. Athanasius.

St Leo the Great 440-461: In 449 Letter to Bishop Flavian of Constantinople he wrote that in Christ, the nature of the mother was assumed, but not her fault. He thus denied the Immaculate Conception— however, the Immaculate Conception was not defined yet, therefore he was not a heretic.

Pope Pelagius I 556-561: 557 Encyclical, *Vas Electiones*: "mainly the venerable bishops, Theodoretus (Cyprus) and Ebus (Adessa) whom I venerate among the orthodox." St. Gregory the Great said they were anathema DS[*] 472; Chalcedon in 451 said they were orthodox in the text of the council not in a canon. Second Council of Constantinople in Canon 13.14 mentions "their godless writings" DS 436.

Pope Honorius I 625-638: "We confess the one will of our Lord Jesus Christ". At this time the two wills of Christ was already doctrine. But if Christ had one will, then He is not God. DS 487. The Third Council of Constantinople condemned him in 681 DS 550 ff. NB— Honorius is condemned by a council, yet in *Anuario Pontefico*, he is still listed. (This is the complete list of the Popes)

Pope St. Nicholas I (the Great) 858-867: Contradicted defined doctrine. Quoting St. Ambrose, he told the bishops of the Bulgarians that it is acceptable to baptize in the name of Christ alone, if a pagan is baptized in the Name of Christ, he need not be rebaptized. Popes Pelagius I, 558; Gregory the Great, 601; Gregory VII, 726; Zacharius, 748; and Stephen II, 754 all defined baptism with the Triune formula. St. Ambrose used Romans 3:6 "I baptized

---

[*] DS refers to Denzinger-Schonmetzer which is a Catholic resource that has doctrinal, conciliar, and papal quotations and definitions. I use this throughout.

in the name of Christ", but here St. Paul was only using short hand. How could St. Nicholas say such a horrid thing?

Pope John VIII 872-882: Methodius brought the Slavonic liturgy which used the vernacular against papal decrees. Pope John finally blessed him and said it was acceptable. Thus we have a new language inserted into the liturgy.

Pope Stephen VI 896-897: Had the body of Pope Formosus dug up, stripped and thrown in the Tiber. His body was recovered and buried after the "divesting ceremony" that also cut off his canonical digits.

Pope Sergius III 904-911: Let the wife of Count Fruscati, Theodora, and then later her daughter Marotia, actually control the papacy. This affected multiple popes including Leo VI, 928; Stephen VII, 929-931; John XI, 931-935 (John was the son of Marotia, who was not elected but only placed there).

John XII 955-964: Drove his predecessor John XI out of Rome, then was such a bad pope that Emperor Otto I came down from Germany to take care of him and made him swear an oath to do his duty, the Oath of Incoronation. John signed it. The moment the Emperor left Rome, John went back to his old ways. Leo VIII took over. NB— still all these men are listed as popes. Also, John XI came back with a vengeance, and Leo had to flee.

Benedict IX 1032-1044: The Romans were so sick of him they chased him away. Bishop John of Sabena bought the Papacy from Benedict, becoming Pope Sylvester III, reigning from Jan 1045 to March 1045, until Benedict IX came back with a vengeance from March 1045 to May 1045. Then Sylvester III was sent back to Sabena. Benedict IX sold the papacy again, this time to the arch-priest of St. Mary Majors, who became Gregory VI some time in 1045 to 1046. In 1046 a pseudo-synod of Sutry under the Emperor called Sylvester a non-Pope and Gregory was called a non-Pope. The Emperor nominated the Bishop of Branburg, who became Clement II. But Benedict came back a third time until 1048. The Emperor intervened again and put in Damasus II in 1048 and died the same year.

<u>Pope Victor II 1048-1057</u>: Appointed by Emperor St. Henry II.

<u>St. Gregory VII 1073-1085</u>: Wrote *"Dictatus Pape"* which tried to explain to the Emperor that he had no right to do anything: "the relationship between the emperor and the Pope is like the Lord and His swineherd". Henry IV was forced to stand and kneel in the snow. The prestige of the papacy fell drastically, because he also wrote that "every single pope, the moment he is validly elected, through the merits of St. Peter, is made a saint". Here we have obvious heresy about grace where he is essentially saying that papal election is an eighth sacrament and makes a saint. Gregory was named a saint in the 17th century when the popes wanted to raise their prestige. But this was not a good idea.

Between 1268-1271, there was no pope.

<u>Pope Boniface VIII 1294-1303</u>: Very arrogant, insulted a cripple, midgets, one-legged, etc. Any money or goods which he could lay his hands on, he took. *"Unam Sanctam"*, 1302: Theory of the two swords, denied Emperor of temporal reign. Leo XIII corrected this. In the "Sanctions", Boniface said that whoever contradicts him is a Manichean, and also that it is necessary to be a subject of the pope to be saved. This was used as a means by satan to destroy the Church. It was prophesied at this time that the fallen would try to use obedience to destroy the Church.

<u>Clement V 1305-1314</u>: Stayed in Avignon which lasted for 70 years, but the Pope is the Bishop of Rome. It is an error to say the pope is infallible in his pastoral actions. A Bishop has to stay in his see to rule it.

<u>John XXII 1316-1334</u>: A learned and saintly man, erred by saying the souls of dead could not receive the beatific vision (Go to heaven) until the last judgment. He withdrew this on his deathbed, December 4, 1334, leaving it to his successor to figure out. Benedict XII in 1336 said the souls of the dead go to Heaven, Hell, or Purgatory.

Urban VI 1378-1389: His personality was so disgusting that the cardinals declared his election invalid at Avignon and elected Antipope Clement VII, 1378-1394. St. Catherine of Siena said Urban was pope and Clement was the Devil's stooge. St. Vincent Ferrer said the opposite.

Boniface IX reigned 1389-1404; Innocent VII reigned 1404-1406; Gregory XII reigned 1406-1415 while the Avignon line continued: after Clement VII, Antipope Benedict XIII reigned 1394-1417, and then in 1409 a Council of Pisa declared the Popes in Rome and Avignon popes and elected Alexander V. He reigned 1409-1410, then John XXIII reigned 1410-1415. At this time there were there popes and three emperors at the same time. Needless to say, people thought it was the last judgment. In 1414 the Council of Constance (historically called the council of Florence) was called and all three popes were treated equally, thus saying that a council was above the pope, which is heresy. In 1417, Antipope Benedict XIII of the Avignon line abdicated, and then Martin V reigned 1417-1431. He was followed by Eugene IV 1431-1447, and both signed the "Conciliar Heresy" that said in a church crisis or schism a council is above a pope.

Rotten Popes

Innocent VIII 1484-1492: legitimized his children, thus ridiculing celibacy (Hilliare Bellock), and had their weddings in the papal palace.

Alexander VI 1492-1503: Did the same as Innocent above.

Pius III reigned for two months in 1503, and then was followed by Julius II, a good pope, who reigned 1503-1513.

Leo X 1513-1523: Did the same as Innocent and Alexander above.

Clement VII 1523-1534: Nephew of Leo X. Had a good lifestyle but is called the most infelicitous in church history: He was a timid Medici that would not make a decision, flip-flopped often. When he became pope, Europe was completely Catholic, but when he died one third of it was protestant. Pathetic.

Paul IV 1555-1559: Interrupted the Council of Trent. He was pious, but arrogant and insane about his "papal dignity", and also very paranoid. He made his nephew the Secretary of State who then stole everything he could get his hands on, but Paul wouldn't hear of it, would not even receive anyone that spoke this way. Pius XII was the next pope that refused his own cardinals. One poor cardinal was called to see the pope, then locked up and never knew why he was suspected of heresy. Paul IV wrote the Bull "*Cum Exopostolics Officero*" that said a former heretic could not be pope. But this bull is a dead letter: the next pope who wrote about papal elections didn't even mention it, and Leo XIII contradicted it by making the former heretic John Henry Newman a Cardinal, thus eligible for the papacy. The Roman Inquisition at this time was used by people to remove enemies and became corrupt. The pope is bound by canon law; he can change it, but he must follow it.

Clement XIV dissolved the Jesuits, and then Pius VII brought them back. Thus showing a pastoral act.

Pius IX 1854: Authored *Innefabilese Deus* which has error in the Sanctions: "should therefore, which God may prevent, some dare to think in their heart otherwise than what we have defined, so that they may recognize and know further, that they are judged by their own sentence, have lost their faith and their unity with the church." But all the other councils say "*si quis dixeris*" (if one was to say). This contradicts Trent DS 1814: about the hidden things the church does not judge. A pope has no right to judge the thoughts of the faithful. Thus, 16 years before infallibility is pronounced, we see the limits of infallibility. But the church is a visible institution, not invisible.

Pius XI 1922-1939: Oct 7, 1930, Filioque was omitted because Russians were present, by Pius XI. He was corrected by the Prefect for the Congregations of Rites. The pope slammed his fist on the table three times saying it was his policy, thus we see "*ost politic*": the sacrificing of Catholic Doctrine for the sake of getting along.

Pius XII 1939-1958: "*Mediator Dei 37*" changed the oldest liturgical principle in the Church from 250: "*Leget credendi lex statuat suplicandi*" (the law of what has to be prayed may determine the law of what has to be believed). Example: Immaculate Conception in Dec 8, 1854, became a law of what has to be believed. Pius confused his authority; the Church alone may govern the liturgy. He said that he may govern the liturgy. *Humani Generis,* 1950: "But if the supreme pontiffs in their official acts purposely pass judgment on a matter debated until then, it is obvious to all, according to the mind and will of the same pontiffs, the matter cannot be considered any longer a question open to free discussion among theologians." But what about all the mistakes above listed? They were all official acts. This would mean that the "ordinary" judgment of the pope is infallible. Of course this is nonsense.

St. John Bosco: "The pope is god on earth, Christ has set the pope above the prophets, his precursor, above the angels, Christ has set the pope on the same level with God."

No wonder there are so many sedevacantists; the popes have to be saints, if not…

The Oath of Incoronation
-Boniface VIII 1302: last to sign this oath (signed his own name); 678 Pope St. Agotho I: the first to sign it.
-For 600 years it was signed and sent to the emperor. But no pope contradicted this solemn act and it is still in the *Libertiunus* today.
-*Libertiunus Honorum Pontificum* has all the details of Papal specifics (*Urbi et Orbi*, papal mass etc.).
"I ____ swear that I will not reduce, change, or permit anything new in anything that I found in my God-pleasing predecessors. Rather, to conserve reverently with glowing devotion as their faithful pupil and successor with all of my power the handed down deposit. To cleanse everything that might arise in contradiction of canonical order. To safeguard the laws and holy canons of our Popes as divine instructions from Heaven. Since I am conscious that I will have to give strictest justification about everything that I confess at the Divine Judgment and to You Whose place I possess through Divine grace and whose Vicariate I

occupy with Your support. Should I undertake to act in anything in another sense, or should I permit that this is done, then You will not show Your mercy to me on that terrible day of the Divine Judgment."

(In the letter, now the pope would write)

"Therefore we submit also to the exclusion under the strictest ban whomsoever might dare, whether it is us, or anyone else, to undertake anything new or in contradiction to the suchlike evangelical tradition and the purity of the Orthodox faith and the Christian religion, or who should attempt through his adversarial efforts to change anything or to hide anything from the purity of the faith or to agree with whomsoever should agree to undertake such a blasphemous audacity."

This is what the Church thinks about the Pope:

Limits to papal power:

Thus the rule of the Pope is quite limited, and the most heretical terrible popes are counted as popes. The pope has no ability to go against natural law. Black is not white, sorry St. Ignatius of Loyola. The pope cannot say vices are virtues, sorry St. Belarmine. But St. Belarmine did say the pope can fall into heresy, unjust laws of the pope do not bind in conscience, the pope is neither the temporal ruler of the world nor the Christian world, he has the supreme temporal power indirectly only (keep the Ten Commandments).

Limit of Divine law: The pope cannot change the sacraments (Innocent III said if the pope changed the rites of the sacraments he would put himself outside the Church); St. Bernard of Clarvioux, *De consideratione* book 4, 23: "You are the mother not the mistress of other churches, you are not the lord of bishops but one of their number." Point here is that the pope has the last word.

Limit through Ecclesiastical law: Moral theology teaches that the legislator is subject to his own laws, if not by coercive powers, at least in the manner of the directive. Precepts that are unjust now, harmful, do not require obedience, except in the case of avoiding scandal (If it is an unimportant thing).

164

Dogmatic Limits: He cannot define what is in no way related to revelation (for example, "Toyota makes the best SUV"). He has to stick to tradition, no novelty. And he is bound to the teachings of his predecessors.

Practical Limits: politics, disease, blackmail, stupidity, vice, etc.

Seven Ages of the Church
Inspired by Blessed Fr. Bartholomew Holtzhauser

1st 33-70 <u>Age of the Apostles</u> (age of sowing)
    St. Thomas died in India
    St. Bartholomew in Armenia
    St. Andrew died in Greece
    Sts. Peter and Paul in Rome
    St. James the Greater died in Spain

2nd 71-313 <u>Age of the Martyrs</u> (age of blood)
    10 Roman persecutions Nero to Diocletian
    Romans practiced ecumenism, Catholics said no
    Battle of Milvian Bridge, Constantine vs. Maxentius
      "in this sign you will conquer" Px = Chr the first three
      letters of Christ

3rd 314-500ish <u>Age of the Doctors</u> (age of learning)
    The fallen change their plans, now they attack minds with
    heresy
      -nestorian, arian, monophysite, palagian, donatist
      Four Greek Doctors - Gregory of Nissa, Gregory of
        Nansiansus, Basil, Athanasius
    Three Latin - Ambrose, Augustine, Jerome
      (Gregory the Great comes a little later)
      St Chrysostom (Greek)
        -the great creeds are developed

4th 500ish-1517 <u>Age of Christendom</u> (age of teaching)
    1000 years when Christ was in control of civilization, the
    world was Christian, nations were converting, great buildings,
    cathedrals
    St. Thomas 1200, soon after him the decline begins, Duns
    Scotus contradicts everything. Maybe a jealousy of the
    Franciscans against the Dominicans.
    1400 St. Vincent Ferrer, so disgusted by the decadence of the
    age, thought the end of the world was near. But he slowed the
    decline.

St. Joan of Arc - mission to restore the French King, crowned in Reims to reestablish proper authority. Lasted until 1789-king's head chopped in 1792.

5th 1517- ? <u>Age of Apostasy and Hypocrisy</u> (Emperor Charles V- Rise of the Great Monarch/Chastisement)
> Repeated attacks
>> 1517-denied the Church, believed in Christ and God
>> 1717- liberalism, Masonry, denied Church, Christ, believed in God
>> 1917- communism, Masonry in Action, denied Church, Christ, and God
>
> Everyone knows Christ but wants to dance with the devil, protestants act as a reform but really a deform, liberals nice guys until you disagree, communists are worse— they force all to become communist or kill them.
> 1965 Vat II the logical end of the Age of Apostasy, the Great Apostasy
>> This marks to the end of the Tridentine Church, Trent
>> Also the end of the Constantinian Church = the unity of the state and church

6th ? <u>Age of Peace</u>, Age of Our Lady's Triumph of Her
> Immaculate Heart (from the time of the Chastisement to the 7th age)
> Major intervention of God, Who is the only One Who can clean this mess up.
> Practically all the world will be Catholic; England, Russia, and China will convert

7th will begin the corruptions
> AntiChrist— he will make war on three kingdoms of the ten and will bring terrible persecutions

Endnotes

[i] Aristotle. *Physics* 195 a 6–8. Cf. *Metaphysics* 1013 b 6–9

[ii] Horvat, Marian Therese. *Our Lady of Good Success: Prophesies for our times.* Los Angeles. Tradition in Action, Inc. Sixth edition 2020.

[iii] LaSalette.org

[iv] Lourdes-France.org

[v] Ullathorne, William Bernard. *The Holy Mountain of La Salette, Pilgrimage of the year 1854.* London. Richardson and Son. 1854.

[vi] Koster, John P. *The Atheist Syndrome.* Brentwood, TN. Wolgemuth & Hyatt. 1989.

[vii] Bishop O'Gara wrote this little 25 page pamphlet after returning to the USA. He had been in a CCP prison for two years. The Passionist Order has it in their archives: passioinistarchives.org

[viii] Galton, Francis. *Hereditary Genius: An Inquiry into Its Laws and Consequences.* London. Macmillan and Co. 1869.

[ix] Sanger, Margaret. *Woman and the New Race.* New York. Brentano's. 1920.

[x] Bernhardi, Freidrich von. *Germany and the Next War.* San Francisco. University Press of the Pacific. 2001.

[xi] Much of the details about Our Lady of Fatima in this chapter was found at fatima.org

[xii] English translation of text in Sister Lucy, "Fourth Memoir", *Fatima in Lucia's Own Words.* (Postulation Centre, Fatima, Portugal, 1976) p. 162.

[xiii] English translation of text in Sister Lucy, "Third Memoir", *Fatima in Lucia's Own Words*, p. 104. See also *The Whole Truth About Fatima*, Volume I, p. 182.

[xiv] English translation of text in Sister Lucy, "Fourth Memoir", *Fatima in Lucia's Own Words.* (Postulation Centre, Fatima, Portugal, 1976) p. 162.

[xv] Frère François de Marie des Anges, *Fatima: Intimate Joy World Event*, Book One: *The Astonishing Truth.* (English edition, Immaculate Heart Publications, Buffalo, New York, 1993) pp. 172-173.

[xvi] *O Seculo*, article of October 15, 1917.

[xvii] Frère Michel de la Sainte Trinité, *The Whole Truth About Fatima*, Volume I, p. 340. See also Father John de Marchi, I.M.C., *Fatima From the Beginning*. (Missoes Consolata, Fatima, Portugal, 1981, third edition, first published in 1950) p. 141; and Joseph A Pelletier, A.A., *The Sun Dances at Fatima*. (Doubleday, New York, 1983) pp. 129-130.

[xviii] John M. Haffert, *Meet the Witnesses*. (AMI International Press, Fatima, Portugal, 1961) p. 62.

[xix] de Chardin, Pierre Teilhard, *Christianity and Evolution*. New York. Houghton Mifflin Harcourt Publishing Company. 1969.

[xx] Belloc, Hilaire. *The Great Heresies*. London, Sheed and Ward. 1938.

[xxi] 2018 *The Barque of Paul* ("*La barca di Paolo*"), by Fr. Leonardo Sapienza, regent of the Pontifical Household.

[xxii] Eudes, St. John. *The Priest, His Dignity and Obligations*. Fitzwilliam, NH, Loreto Publications, 2008.

[xxiii] http://www.catholictradition.org/Mary/akita.htm

[xxiv] https://www.ewtn.com/catholicism/library/message-from-our-lady--akita-japan-5167

[xxv] https://aleteia.org/2019/05/14/our-lady-of-akitas-powerful-message-to-the-modern-world

Made in the USA
Las Vegas, NV
07 December 2022

61185792R00098